GEOFF BOYCOTT'S CRICKET QUIZ BOOK

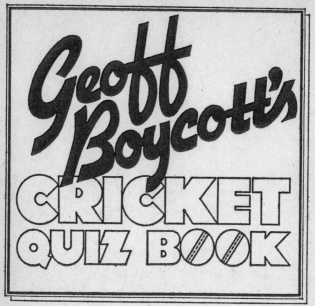

Geoff Boycott's CRICKET QUIZ BOOK

Edited by
BARRIE J. TOMLINSON

MIRROR BOOKS

© Geoff Boycott
First published in 1979 by Mirror Books Ltd.,
Athene House, 66–73 Shoe Lane, London EC4P 4AB,
for Mirror Group Newspapers Ltd.
Printed in the UK by
Hunt Barnard Printing Ltd., Aylesbury, Bucks

ISBN 0 85939 152 3

CONTENTS

	Page
The Schweppes County Championship	8
John Player League	14
The Gillette Cup	18
Tests v. India	22
Tests v. Pakistan	26
Tests v. West Indies	30
Tests v. Australia	34
Tests v. New Zealand	40
World Cup	44
Batsmen	48
Bowlers	54
Wicket-keepers	60
The Counties	64
Derbyshire	64
Essex	66
Glamorgan	68
Gloucestershire	70
Hampshire	72
Kent	74
Lancashire	76
Leicestershire	78
Middlesex	80
Northamptonshire	82
Nottinghamshire	84
Somerset	86
Surrey	88
Sussex	90
Warwickshire	92
Worcestershire	94
Yorkshire	96
Records	98
Dates	102
Rules	106
My Section	116
Season 1978	122
True or False	128
Benson & Hedges Cup	134

INTRODUCTION (BY GEOFF BOYCOTT)

Perhaps more than any other sport, cricket ideally lends itself to fill the pages of a book such as this. For cricket is truly a statistician's delight. Whereas most sports are over in a matter of hours, cricket can be played for up to five days at Test match level and during that time, lots of things happen which make good quiz questions!

I hope you enjoy going through the various sections of this book. I am sure you will find some of the questions too easy and some too hard . . . but I quickly discovered that it was going to be impossible to please everybody!

Take this book with you when you go to watch your favourite team in action. If the weather intervenes and rain or bad light stops play, you can always pass the time testing yourself, or a friend, on your knowledge of cricket.

Quizzes and crosswords often occupy the time players spend in the pavilion. Indeed, I have known many of my team-mates to have competitions to see who could complete *The Times* crossword in the fastest time. I don't usually enter crossword competitions . . . but I rather fancy my chances on cricket questions, for not only has my daily contact with the sport given me a good all-round knowledge, I also have a fine collection of old cricket books, which fans have been kind enough to send me over the years . . . and they are packed with facts and figures!

As well as questions about English cricketers and events, you'll also find lots of questions about overseas players, for cricket is truly an international sport and players from many different countries are popular and well known, perhaps even more than in their own countries. In sports like soccer, foreign players are usually only noted at the time of World Cup competitions and European Cup matches ... but in cricket, overseas players have been part of the English county scene for many years ... so it is only right they have a big share of this book.

Opening the batting for England, against such fine bowlers as Jeff Thomson, Rodney Hogg and Andy Roberts, is tough enough. But knowing the amount of work that has gone into the preparation of this book, I think I've found a job which is almost as hard! To the best of my knowledge, the facts in this book were correct at the beginning of 1979. But cricket is an all-the-year round sport and somewhere in the world, a match is always taking place and new records are being made, which might just possibly invalidate one or more of the questions and answers in the book. I just hope that if a record is going to change, for the better, then it's me who makes that record ... then I wouldn't mind the book being wrong!

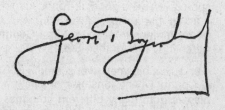

SCHWEPPES COUNTY CHAMPIONSHIP

The County Cricket Championship has been contested for over one hundred years, and there are now seventeen counties taking part. How much do YOU know about the 'backbone' of first-class cricket in this country? Let's find out!

1. Can you name the year the County Championship first began?

2. In the year that qualification rules were first agreed, there was a tied result. Who were the two counties involved?

3. Which county won the title in 1978?

4. Who holds the record for the most consecutive County Championship appearances? He played for Sussex.

5. Yorkshire have won the Championship a record 31 times. But do you know which county has won it the second-highest number of times?

6. When was the last time two counties tied for the Championship?

7. Can you name the Joint Champions in that year?

8. To the nearest fifty, can you say what is the record innings total scored in a County Championship match? (It's more than 800!)

9. Has a batsman ever scored 3,000 runs in a season of County Championship matches?

10. Four counties have scored 800 or more in a single innings in Championship matches. Which ones?

Below are the initials of some very famous county cricketers, both past and present. Can you supply the missing letters of their surnames in each case?

D.B. _ _ _ _ _

D.C.S. _ _ _ _ _ _

M.C. _ _ _ _ _ _

I.T. _ _ _ _ _

M.H. _ _ _ _ _ _

F.S. _ _ _ _ _ _

On this page are eleven jumbled letters, a real mixed-up cricketer from the past. Everybody knows him, but here are three clues.

1. He was a right-handed bowler.

2. He made his county debut at the age of 18.

3. He set a Test record by taking 307 wickets.

R U F
R T A
D E E M
N

1. Who achieved an analysis of 10 for 10 in 1932, and which county did he play for?

2. Who was the last Warwickshire player to captain England?

3. Who holds the double record of scoring more runs and making most hundreds in first-class matches than any other batsman? (He played for Surrey.)

4. One county won the Championship title for seven consecutive years, an incredible achievement. First, name the county.

5. And now give the years, please!

6. Back in 1907, one county scored only 12 runs in an innings. Do you know which it was?

7. A Kent batsman scored two double centuries in a County Championship match against Essex in 1938. Who was he?

8. What is the highest first-wicket partnership in County cricket?

9. When was the last time Yorkshire won the Championship?

10. Can you name the first County captain to become a bishop? He played for Sussex.

1. On only one occasion has the County Champion-ship been shared by more than two counties. It was in 1889. Can you name the three Joint Champions?

2. How many counties competed in the first year of the Championship? 9, 16 or 24?

3. Which of the first-class county cricket clubs was formed in 1845.

4. Four counties have never won the Championship. How many of them do you know?

5. Which was the last county to gain admittance to the County Championship?

6. Which English county cricket badge features a bear with a ragged staff?

7. In what year were Yorkshire led by a professional cricketer for the first time this century? They retained the County Championship title.

8. Tony Greig scored his first double-century for Sussex in 1975 with a score of 226. But against which county?

9. When did Leicestershire win the County Championship for the first time? To give you a clue, it was not long ago.

10. Who were known as the 'Terrible Twins' of Middlesex when they played?

Test matches in England are played on six county grounds. Fill in the missing letters to complete the famous names — and also say which counties play on them.

.O. DS

A

T .. N .. R . DG .

L .. . AF . .. RD

E .. . B . S . O .. .

.. . AD .. . G .. Y

THE JOHN PLAYER LEAGUE

1. In which year was the John Player League first played? 1955, 1969 or 1975?

2. Who were the very first champions? Yorkshire, Lancashire or Derbyshire?

3. Which county has won the league the most times? A clue: it's a county near London.

4. Still referring to the previous question, how many times? 3, 4 or 5 times?

5. Out of these teams, only one has not won the John Player League: Worcestershire, Hampshire, Leicestershire, Essex. Which is the odd one out?

6. Who won the League championship in 1978?

7. Another question about the 1978 championship – who was captain of the winning side? Fill in the missing letters: RICHARD G _ L _ _ A _.

8. What does the winning side receive: a trophy cup; a shield or a statuette?

9 lowest total of a John Player match came to 23 , between LIMDEDESX and KEIYROHRS. Unjumble the letters to name the two teams.

10. Here is the result of the highest match aggregate – 525 runs – which happened in 1975: _ O _ E _ S _ T (270) and _ _ OU _ _ ST _ _ SH _ _ E (255). Fill in the missing letters to name the two teams.

It's always a shame for the runners-up, because they almost made it but not quite. Starting at the top and taking a letter from each segment, you should know the John Player runners-up in 1978.

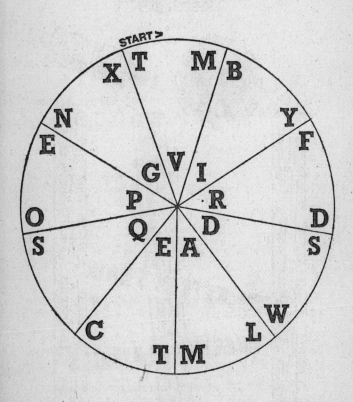

In 1970, A. Ward set a John Player League bowling record, that was a fantastic achievement. Among the three sets of figures on this page is the actual record he achieved. Can you guess which is the correct one?

4 WICKETS IN 5 BALLS

5 WICKETS IN 4 BALLS

4 WICKETS IN 4 BALLS

1. How many points does a winning side in the John Player League get? 2, 3 or 4 points?

2. How many points does a team get in the event of a tie? 2; 1 or no points?

3. A John Player match consists of one innings per side. But how many overs does each innings consist of — 30; 40 or 60 overs?

4. In 1977, a world-famous West Indian cricketer set a new John Player League record by hitting the greatest number of sixes in a season. Who was he?

5. B. A. Richards made the highest batting score in 1970, in a Hants v. Yorks match. What was the number of runs: 115; 125 or 135? Have a guess if you're not sure!

6. In 1971, the match between Essex and Northamptonshire lasted for 2 hours 13 minutes . . . what was significant about the match? There's a clue in the time!

7. C. E. B. Rice, playing for Nottinghamshire, scored the most runs in a season, in 1977. How many runs? The answer is one of these figures: 706; 799; 814.

8. 190 runs was the biggest victory ever and it happened in 1973, in a match between Kent and Northamptonshire. But which team beat which?

9. The most wickets ever got by a bowler during a season was in 1974, when R. J. Clapp took 34 wickets. Which team was Clapp playing for then? Unjumble the letters for the answer: MTRESEOS.

10. Australia has its own John Player League . . . true or false?

THE GILLETTE CUP

The Gillette Cup is a knock-out competition which started in 1963 and is competed for by the seventeen first-class counties, and the five leading Minor counties during the previous season. Let's see how much you know about it . . .

1. The Final is always played at the same ground. Which one?

2. Each Gillette Cup match consists of one innings per side. But how many overs is it limited to?

3. Name the county who won the trophy in 1963, its first year?

4. In which year did Middlesex win the Gillette Cup?

5. Now can you say which county won the Cup competition three years in succession?

6. Who holds the record for the highest individual score in Gillette Cup matches?

7. David Sydenham of Surrey achieved a unique Gillette Cup bowling performance in 1964. Do you know what it was?

8. Some more bowling figures. In the history of the competition, how many bowlers have taken seven wickets in an innings?

9 Which three counties share the unfortunate record of the lowest Gillette Cup total of only 41?

10. Kent won the competition in 1978. True or False?

Below is a circle. In each section is hidden a county which has won the Gillette Cup in the last fifteen years. Unscramble the letters to get the correct answers.

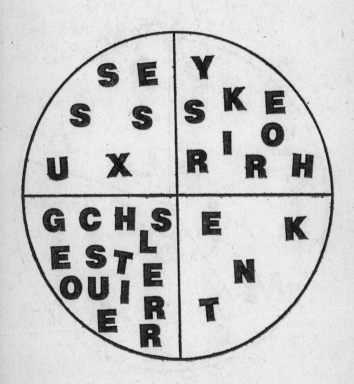

A brilliant batsman who plays Gillette Cup cricket for Lancashire is hidden below. Take one letter of the three in each segment of the circle and you'll discover him. A clue – his first name is Clive.

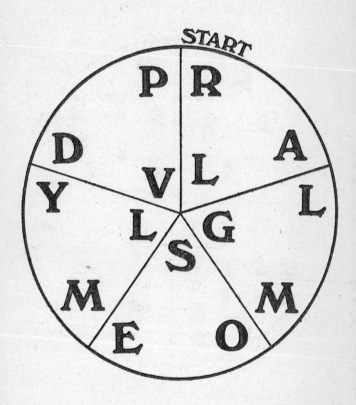

Now for some Gillette Cup alternatives. Only one answer is correct in each case. Is it (a) or (b)?

1. Many centuries have been scored in the competition since it began. Have there been (a) more than 75, or (b) less?

2. Because of bad weather, a Gillette Cup match was once played over only 15 overs. (a) true, or (b) false?

3. Essex won the competition in (a) 1975, or (b) never?

4. Basil D'Oliveira of Worcestershire has been named the 'Man of the Match' on (a) six occasions, or (b) two?

5. A dog once stopped play in a Gillette Cup match for twenty minutes. (a) true, or (b) false?

6. The record wicket partnership in a Gillette Cup match is (a) 227, or (b) 160?

7. Is it true that the Final in 1977 started with only one umpire? (a) yes, or (b) no?

8. Leicestershire beat Staffordshire by a record margin in 1975. Was it (a) 299 runs, or (b) 214 runs?

9. A batsman named Mike Llewellyn hit a six in a Gillette Cup match which struck the commentary box. (a) true, or (b) false?

10. Yorkshire have been triumphant in the Gillette Cup Final on (a) one occasion, or (b) two occasions?

TESTS v. INDIA

Perhaps England playing India does not have the tremendous excitement and rivalry of an Australian Test match . . . but it can still test your cricketing knowledge to the full! Try some of these questions for size and you'll see.

1. In which year did India play its first official Test Match? 1929, 1932 or 1937?

2. In 1967, J. T. Murray dismissed a record number of Indian batsmen in an innings at Lord's. How many?

3. What is the lowest number of runs an Indian touring side has made against England? You have a choice of 36 or 42.

4. One of the following has NOT played for India. (a) Umrigar, (b) Mankad, (c) Engineer, (d) Iqbal. Can you choose the odd man out?

5. A famous Indian test bowler has the forenames of Bhagwat Subrahmanya. What is his better-known final name?

6. V. Mankad is the batsman who holds the record for the highest individual innings for India. How many runs did he score? (a) 231, (b) 301, (c) 289, (d) 199?

7. V. Mankad and P. Roy scored a record first-wicket partnership of 413 runs. True or False?

8. Two bowlers have taken nine wickets in an innings for India. S. P. Gupte was one, but who was the other? To give you a clue, it's a common Indian name!

9. How many batsmen 'carried their bats' through innings for India in official Tests before 1976?

10. Two all-rounders scored a century and took five wickets in an innings in the same game for India. They were M _ _ K _ D and UM _ _ _ _ R. Can you complete the names?

With the three sets of blanks on this page, we give you the first and last letters of Indian cricketers in each case. Can you fill the remaining blanks?

B _ _ I

R _ Y

E _ _ _ _ _ _ R

Indian Test Match cricket is not played at two of the following places. Which two?

BOMBAY

KANPUR

MADRAS

CALCUTTA

KARACHI

LAHORE

1. The highest innings ever scored by India is 539. Is that statement true or false?

2. Mulvantrai Himmatial are the forenames of a famous Indian all-rounder. What is he better known as?

3. In which season did India gain its first Test victory over England in England? 1952, 1965 or 1971?

4. And now a different one, particularly if you're not Indian! Who was the captain of that winning Indian side? A. L. W _ _ _ _ _ _ _.

5. Who set a record for an Indian batsman by scoring 774 runs in 1971?

6. A famous former England captain was born in Bangalore, India. Do you know who it was?

7. Gymkhana, the Brabourne Stadium and the Wankhede Stadium are all grounds that have staged Test Matches. In what place in India?

8. Bombay set a world record for winning a first-class championship for the most seasons in succession. How many seasons was it? 3, 15 or 20?

9. The Nawab of Pataudi once played cricket for India. True or False?

10. Do you know how many Test Match centres there are in India?

TESTS v. PAKISTAN

Pakistan are really one of the 'newer' cricket powers. Nevertheless, they have their fair share of talent, thrills and interest when it comes to action. See how you get on with some of these questions !

1. Let's start with a unique record. Four brothers have played Test cricket for Pakistan. Wazir, Hanif, Mushtaq, and Sadiq. What is their surname ?

2. Which batsmen shared in a record ninth wicket partnership of 190 against England in 1967 ?

3. Name the first player to complete the double of 1,000 runs and 100 wickets for Pakistan in Test Matches.

4. In 1958, Pakistan set a record for the highest second innings in Test cricket. Was it (a) 657 for 8 declared, or (b) 598 all out ?

5. A Pakistani bowler named Sarfraz Nawaz took a record number of wickets before lunch on his country's tour of Great Britain in 1974. How many ?

6. What honour does cricketer A. H. Kardar hold ?

7. Which English batsman scored the highest individual innings of 278 for England against Pakistan in 1954 ?

8. Has a Pakistani cricketer ever scored a century in each innings of a match against England ?

9. Still on centuries. Can you name two famous England cricketers who have scored a century on their debut against Pakistan in Test matches ?

10. Intikhab Alam has bowled more balls for Pakistan in Tests than anyone else. Has he bowled more than (a) 5,000, (b) 10,000 or (c) 15,000 balls ?

An English bowler took 13 wickets for 71 runs for England against Pakistan in 1974. Unscramble the letters below to find his identity.

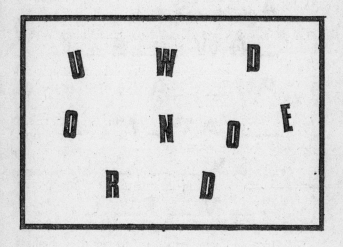

There are six names below – or parts of them anyway. They are all England batsmen who have scored centuries against Pakistan in Test Matches.

A _ _ S _

_ O W _ _ E _

P U _ _ A _

_ _ A V _ N _ _

_ E X _ _ _

C _ M _ T _ _

1. The youngest ever Test player made his debut for Pakistan in 1958/59, at the age of 15 years 124 days. Who was he?

2. There are six Test Match Centres in Pakistan. How many do you know?

3. Pakistan once scored more than 600 runs in a Test innings against England in this country. True or False?

4. What is the lowest innings score Pakistan have made against England? It happened at Lord's in 1954. Was it 42, 102 or 87?

5. M. C. Cowdrey and E. R. Dexter hold a batting record against Pakistan, made in 1962. What is it?

6. Which England bowler has the best figures of 8–51 against Pakistan in this country?

7. In all England v. Pakistan matches so far, what has been the Highest Match Aggregate? (It was more than a thousand!)

8. Who was the captain of the first England touring side of Pakistan in 1961?

9. What World record did Aslam Ali and Khalid Irteza break in October 1975? (Batting.)

10. Pakistan are the only country to win a Test Match during its first rubber in England. True or False?

TESTS v. WEST INDIES

1. First, can you guess the year when the very first Test Match between England and West Indies was played? Was it in 1888, 1928 or 1948?

2. The highest number of runs West Indies have ever had scored against them was set by England at Kingston in 1929–30. Was that score 649, 749 or 849?

3. On which island in the West Indies are the Kingston Test Matches played?

4. In the twenty years from 1957 to 1976, West Indies toured England six times with 1957 and 1976 being two of the years. Give the dates of two of the remaining four tours.

5. Five Tests were played in the 1976 visit by West Indies to England. Two were drawn – who won the other three?

6. On the 1976 tour, West Indies scored their highest ever innings against England – 687 for 8 wickets. Did they achieve this at Lord's, The Oval or Trent Bridge?

7. Who was the England skipper for the 1976 West Indies tour?

8. Up to the end of the 1976 tour, 71 Test Matches had been played between England and West Indies. Of these, 28 were drawn, 22 won by one side and 21 by the other. Which country has had the 22 wins?

9. England v. Australia Tests are played for the Ashes, but do you know which trophy England v. West Indies matches are played for? Is it the Wisden Trophy, the W. J. Jordan Trophy or the Currie Cup?

10. Andy Roberts and Gordon Greenidge were both members of the 1976 West Indies touring side. Do you know for which English county side they have both played?

Pictured on this page is a West Indian cricketer who played seven Tests against England and who also played for Essex. His first name is a good clue, so can you give his surname?

KEITH

Can you fill in the missing letters in the words to spell the names of four cities in the West Indies that are famous as Test Match venues?

B_ _ D _ ET_W_

_EO_GE_O_N

_I_GST_N

_O_T _F _PA_ _

1. Frank Hayes scored a Test debut century against the West Indies in 1973 at the Oval. What county side was Frank playing for at the time?

2. A player was recalled to the England team for the 1976 First Test, after a 9-year break. Was that player: Ray Illingworth, Freddie Trueman, Brian Close or Fred Titmus?

3. True or false? Only one hat-trick has been achieved by a bowler in the 71 Tests between England and West Indies.

4. One of the following players did not play for England on the 1976 West Indies tour: Chris Old, Derek Underwood, Derek Randall, Mike Selvey, Mike Hendrick. Which is the odd man out?

5. One of the greatest West Indian players of all time was Gary Sobers, who skippered them in three Test series against England. But do you know which English county side appointed him captain in 1968?

6. Gary Sobers also holds the record for the most West Indian centuries against England. Can you guess if the record is 8, 10, 12 or 14?

7. Which well-known Northamptonshire player scored a century in the First Test of the 1976 tour?

8. The world record for the number of balls sent down by one bowler in a single innings was set up by Sonny Ramadhin, when playing for West Indies against England at Edgbaston, May–June 1957. Can you guess if he bowled 78, 88, 98 or 108 overs?

9. In the 1976 Third Test, England were bowled out for their lowest ever innings total against West Indies. Was that total: 51, 61, 71 or 81?

10. GONTILRIHLW is the jumbled up surname of an England skipper who led his side in a series against West Indies. Can you name him?

3

TESTS v. AUSTRALIA

The Ashes! There is something compelling, magnetic about the trophy for which all Test Matches between England and Australia are played. It all started so many years ago ... but how knowledgeable are you NOW?

1. Name the year when the Ashes were first contested between the two countries.

2. Who scored his maiden 50 in first-class cricket during a Test Match in 1975? (He was an Aussie.)

3. Who was the first non-wicket-keeper to take 100 catches for Australia in official Tests?

4. Do you know the name of the first Australian, an all-time great, to score 300 runs in a Test Match in a single day?

5. In March 1974, Greg Chappell set a new record for the most runs in a Test Match. How many did he score?

6. Don Bradman holds the record for scoring the fastest double-century in Test cricket? How long did it take him?

7. Who took eight for 84 and eight for 53 in his first Test Match. His initials were R. A. L.

8. Surrey's Jim Laker had a fantastic match against the Australians at Old Trafford in 1956. What was his final analysis?

9. G. L. Jessop scored 100 in 75 minutes at The Oval in which year? 1902, 1922, 1932?

10. In 1903, a batsman scored a total of 306 runs in his maiden Test Match. Can you name him?

There are five Test Match Centres in Australia. Unscramble each section to find them.

LDAEIDEA

ANEBBSRI

EOURLBNEM

ERTPH

YDESNY

Fill in the gaps again ! Get busy with the missing letters and you'll find famous captains in England-Australia Test Matches.

_ R _ C _

Y _ R _ L _ Y

_ L _ I _ G W _ _ _ _ _

_ E N _ _ D

B _ _ D M _ N

C _ A P _ _ L _

B _ E _ _ L E _

1. A former Lord Mayor of Brisbane became head groundsman for the First Test between Australia and England in 1974. Yes or No?

2. Trevor Bailey of Essex holds an unusual record against Australia. What is it?

3. What is the longest time a batsman has gone without scoring a run for England? It was in 1946.

4. A highest innings total, 903-7 declared, was achieved at The Oval. When and by which country?

5. England beat Australia by the largest margin ever in Test cricket in 1938. What was it?

6. What is the highest individual innings made by an England batsman against Australia?

7. How many centuries did Don Bradman score against England in Test Matches?

8. W. H. Ponsford and D. G. Bradman hold the record for the highest 2nd wicket stand for Australia against England. Did they score 389 runs, 420 runs or 451 runs?

9. Has a bowler ever taken all ten wickets in an innings in an England-Australia Test Match?

10. Bowler L. O. Fleetwood-Smith conceded a lot of runs for just one wicket against England at The Oval in 1938. Do you know how many? Was it 298, 398 or 498?

Another circle full of jumbled letters. This time the names are all well-known bowlers who have played either for England or Australia. Sort them out into their correct order.

1. Greg Chappell of Australia holds the record for the most catches in a match against England. How many?

2. Do you know the lowest Innings total ever made by England against Australia? It was a long time ago!

3. In 1977, when Australia came to England, a certain Geoffrey Boycott had a batting average of 147.33 in Test Matches. What was my highest score?

4. Who was top of the bowling averages for England against Australia in 1977? His average was 19.77 if that helps.

5. Don Bradman made an all-time record in a Test series in 1930. How many runs did he score? Was it 874, 974, 1074?

6. What is the highest Innings score ever made by Australia against England? 657, 758, 729?

7. Did Fred Trueman ever get a hat-trick against Australia?

8. Wicket-keeper Alan Knott stumped six Australian batsmen in an innings in June 1977. True or False?

9. In what year did Bill Lawry's Australian Touring Team lose a test series by four matches to nil?

10. Bob Woolmer scored the slowest-ever century in the history of England-Australia Tests. How long did it take him?

TESTS v. NEW ZEALAND

1. When did the first ever Test Series between England and New Zealand take place?

2. Up to the end of 1978, how many Tests have both teams played against each other ... 46; 47; 48; 49 or 50?

3. Again, up to the end of 1978, of all the Tests, how many has England won?

4. What was the biggest win by England over New Zealand, in 1974–75? How many runs, and by how many wickets?

5. The lowest total for any innings occurred in 1954–55 when New Zealand managed to get only ? runs. Give the correct figure ... 6, 16, 26, 36 or 46 runs?

6. Who was captain of England for the Test Series against New Zealand in 1962–63 ... Dexter; May; Hutton; Denness or Hammond?

7. Only one Englishman has captained his country three times against New Zealand, in 1969, 1970–71, and 1973. Unjumble the letters to identify him ... ARY GTIWLNIOHRL.

8. In the 1931 Test Series, New Zealand batsman M. Page was the first to achieve something for his country in England ... what was it?

9. Only one of these players has never captained New Zealand in Tests against England ... G. T. Dowling; T. C. Lowry; B. Sutcliffe; M. L. L. Page; B. Sinclair. Who is the odd man out?

10. Prior to 1978, where was the last England v. New Zealand Test Series held ... in New Zealand or England?

Here are the initials of a famous New Zealand cricketer who found more fame playing for Worcestershire. Can you name him?

1978 Test Matches. England v. New Zealand.

1. A shock victory was made by New Zealand in the first match of the first series. By how many runs did they win . . . 35; 42; 72; 83; 90?

2. Brothers Richard and Dayle Hadlee both bowled for New Zealand in the first series. One brother is a fast bowler, the other a medium-pace bowler . . . say which is which.

3. In the 2nd match of the first series, there was a famous incident involving England batsman Derek Randall when he was run out, while backing up, by the New Zealand bowler called . . . ? Boock; Chatfield; Collinge; Cairns?

4. An England player gave a remarkable performance in the first series, 2nd match, scoring 103 runs and taking 8 wickets. Who was the player?

5. In the first series, 3rd match, a New Zealand batsman scored over a hundred in each innings, and became only the second New Zealander to achieve this feat in a Test. Unjumble the letters to spell his name . . . FOGEF RAWOHTH.

6. In the second series, England won the 1st and 2nd matches. Is it true or false that New Zealand won the 3rd match?

7. The award for best player of the second series went to an Englishman. Was it . . . Bob Taylor; Bob Willis; Mike Hendrick; Graham Gooch?

8. In the second series, Bev Congdon set a new Test career record for New Zealand, in . . . batting; bowling or wicket-keeping?

9. Who was the New Zealander who replaced Jock Edwards as wicket-keeper, in the second series? Bruce _ _ _ _ _ _.

10. Young England batsman David Gower made his first ever Test hundred, during the second series . . . in the 1st, 2nd, or 3rd match?

Here, you'll find four New Zealanders who played in the 1978 Test Series against England. Fill in the missing letters or unjumble the letters, to give the surnames!

AN _ _ R _ _ N

BR _ C _ W _ _ L

G T
R W I
H

E R
K R
A P

WORLD CUP

Just as football has a World Cup competition, so does cricket. But it's a much newer tournament than the soccer one. Up to the end of 1978, only one official World Cup cricket tournament had been held, so all the following questions refer to that competition.

1. In which country was the first World Cup tournament held?

2. In which year was the competition first held?

3. Name the two non-Test match playing countries that took part.

4. Not a ball was lost in the whole tournament due to rain or bad light — true or false?

5. Which well-known British Assurance company sponsored the event?

6. How many countries took part in the competition? Was it 4, 8, 12 or 16?

7. The New Zealand captain made the tournament's highest score. Who was he? Was his innings 101, 151, 171 or 191?

8. Who captained India in the competition — S. Venkataraghavan, Bishen Bedi or Farouk Engineer?

9. The countries competed in a series of single innings matches for the trophy. How many overs was each innings limited to — 40, 50 or 60?

10. Which two countries eventually played in the final?

Mixed up in the circle below are the surname and Christian name of the captain of the World Cup winning country. Who is he?

This picture clue spells the name of the ground on which England lost their semi-final match against Australia. Can you work it out?

1. On which ground was the 1975 final played?

2. Did the final end with a catch, lbw or a run-out?

3. One of the following players did not take part in the final – Sir Gary Sobers, Rohan Kanhai, Alvin Kallicharran, Vivian Richards. Which is the odd man out?

4. Who captained England in the tournament?

5. England, Australia and the West Indies were three of the semi-finalists – which country was the fourth?

6. Who was the only bowler to take 6 wickets in an innings in the tournament? Was it Gary Gilmour. Wayne Daniel or Bob Willis?

7. Was the winning margin in the final: 5 wickets, 17 runs or 55 runs?

8. Who scored a century in the final and won the Man of the Match award?

9. Which one of the following players did not play for England during the tournament: Geoff Boycott, Derek Randall, Tony Greig, Derek Underwood, Alan Knott?

10. Name the country that batted first in the final.

BATSMEN

To be a great batsman is probably the dream of most cricketing enthusiasts . . . to possess the skill to whack the ball for a six. What more exhilarating feeling is there? There have been many great batsmen . . . and you'll come across some of the most famous names among the questions over the next six pages.

1. Let's start with a question about the most famous batsman of all time, who played in the Victorian era. Do you know his name? Was it W. G. Mace; W. G. Grace; W. G. Lace; W. G. Pace?

2. Give the name of another very famous batsman. He scored the highest number of runs ever by a batsman in a career, between the years 1905–34. Was he called Jack Hibbs; Jack Hubbs; Jack Hebbs; Jack Hobbs?

3. Another famous batsman of former times was Herbert Sutcliffe, who sadly died recently – but he will never be forgotten. Which nationality was Herbert Sutcliffe – British; Australian or West Indian?

4. Can you identify this great batsman of more modern times? He was captain of Kent for many years, ranging from the 1950's to the 1970's, and also captain of England during some of that time. His son, whose first name is Christopher, now plays for Kent and is a brilliant young batsman. Now name the batsman. He's Colin C _ W _ _ _ Y.

5. Hanif Mohammad batted for 16 hours 10 minutes, the longest innings in first-class cricket. Name his country: New Zealand; South Africa; Pakistan or India?

6. England player Derek Randall is an all-action batsman. Which county does he play for?

7. Name the batsman. He established himself as a regular opening batsman for England, and is a member of the Essex side. Unjumble the letters to find his name . . . RAHGAM OCGHO.

8. This top England batsman has captained Middle-

sex to many victories. Another clue: his first name is Mike. Now give his surname.

9. Brothers Ian and Greg Chappell have both batted for and captained Australia. Which brother took over the captaincy from the other brother?

10. A famous Australian batsman whose cricket career spanned the years 1927–49. Fill in the missing letters to give his surname ... DONALD B _ _ D M A _.

Here's an artist's impression of a famous Essex and England batsman. Can you guess who it is?

In the circle below is the Christian and surname of an England captain who was Cricketer of the Year way back in 1938. A Yorkshireman like me, this very famous batsman was my boyhood hero and is now a Sir !

1. A batsman must use a bat that's no more than 40 inches in length. True or false?

2. A Northamptonshire batsman... when facing bowlers, you can say he has nerves of — ? His first name is David. Now can you say who we're talking about?

3. Another name-puzzler ... sort out the letters to make up the name of a former hard-hitting Sussex batsman DET TEXRED.

4. Give the Christian name of each of the following batsmen ... Greenidge, Kallicharran, McCosker.

5. Tower, Flower, Power... no, not one of those is the surname of this young, up-and-coming England batsmen. But his surname does rhyme with those words. A further clue: David is his first name. Who is it?

6. Ian Botham is, of course, a successful batsman. But he plays another role in cricket just as important. Is that as a wicket-keeper; fielder or bowler?

7. Here's a similar question about Roger Tolchard, also an excellent batsman. What is his other role in cricket: bowler; fielder or wicket-keeper?

8. New Zealand batsman Mike Burgess has never been captain of his country's side. True or false?

9. Which of the following batsmen is the odd one out? Clive Radley, Geoff Miller, Mike Denness, Dennis Amiss?

10. Read the clues and name the batsman. A player for Surrey. Retired from cricket in 1968. Managed the England Test teams on tours abroad. He's KEN B _ _ _ _ _ _ _ _ _.

Here are four leading batsmen of the 1978 home season . . . but they've been joined with the wrong teams. Put them in their correct pairs!

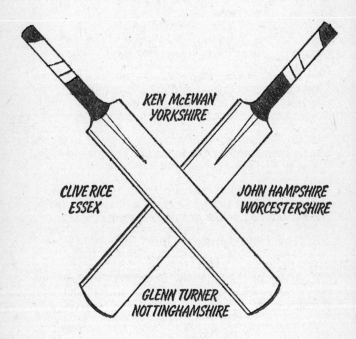

KEN McEWAN
YORKSHIRE

CLIVE RICE
ESSEX

JOHN HAMPSHIRE
WORCESTERSHIRE

GLENN TURNER
NOTTINGHAMSHIRE

What stroke am I playing in this picture?

For some cricket fans, a bowler is the most exciting player on a pitch ... he's the one who attacks and starts any action. Now it's up to you to get to grips with the puzzlers here and show how much you know about bowlers.

1. Fill in the letters:
   Player for Warwickshire ... England, too.
   He bowls fast, that's what he can do.
   Yes, he's the man for that job,
   His surname is W _ _ _ _ _ and his first name is _ _ _ l

2. Mike Hendrick bowls for which county team?

3. An England off-spinner who plays for Derbyshire ... name him!

4. 1978 was a good year for Essex bowler John Lever, when he received an acclaim, being voted − ? Give the name of his award.

5. Unjumble the letters to identify this England and Yorkshire fast bowler ... SCRIH DOL.

6. Middlesex spin-bowler John Emburey has never played in any Test Match for England. True or false?

7. Another bowler for Middlesex is Phil Edmonds. Is he classed as a fast; fast-medium or spin bowler?

8. Kent and England bowler Derek Underwood had the distinction of taking most wickets in the 1978 season. Was that 70; 110; 85; or 94 wickets?

9. Ian Botham has taken countless wickets in county and Test matches. Is he a left handed or right handed bowler?

10. For which county team does Ian Botham play ... Surrey; Leicestershire; Kent; Somerset or Glamorgan?

In the list below, the bowlers are opposite the incorrect teams. Put them in their right pairs!

R. East . . . . Sussex

B. Woolmer . . . . Essex

M. Selvey . . . . Lancashire

H. Moseley . . . . Glamorgan

A. Mack . . . . Kent

R. Ratcliffe . . . . Middlesex

G. Arnold . . . . Somerset

Mixed up in the square below are the names of two famous Australian bowlers. Can you unjumble the letters to discover the names?

T D F I E N
E H N S J
M O L I N S
L O E E F L

1. Can you give the correct name of this famous Indian slow bowler: Bashen Bidi; Boshen Badi; Bishen Bedi; Bushen Budi; Beshen Bidi?

2. Frank Tyson was a great all-time England bowler, who retired some years ago. He went to live in Australia ... is that true or false?

3. Which year? In his very first Test Match for Australia, Bob Massie took an amazing 16 wickets for 137 runs against England in ... 1970; 1972; 1974; 1976 or 1978?

4. Harold Larwood has the credit of bowling the fastest cricket ball measured for speed, in 1933, in England. What was that fastest speed ... 83 mph; 93 mph; 103 mph; 113 mph or 123 mph?

5. The most runs ever conceded by a bowler in a match was 428 by C. S. Nayudu in Bombay, 1945. Can you guess the number of deliveries he made ... 778; 917; 987; 1,222; 1,306?

6. No bowler in first class cricket has ever achieved 5 wickets with 5 consecutive balls. The nearest to it happened in 1922 when Charles Parker hit the stumps with five successive balls ... but the second ball was called invalid. For which reason?

7. Famous TV news announcer Reginald Bosanquet has a connection with the 'googly' bowling ... What is that connection?

8. The fastest bowler of all time is considered to have been Charles Kortright, who lived from 1871 until 1952. Which county did he play for ... Kent; Essex; Gloucestershire; Derbyshire; Sussex?

9. Did New Zealand fast bowler Richard Hadlee play for his country's side in the 1978 Prudential Trophy matches?

10. Bev Congdon is well-known internationally as a top bowler. Which country does he play for ... New Zealand; Australia; England; West Indies?

1. Pakistan's Abdul Qadir ... is he a fast bowler or a spinner?

2. A spin bowler for Pakistan is Qasim ... what is his first name?

3. Which is the odd bowler out ... Sikander Bakht; Imran Khan; Madan Lal; Liaquat Ali?

4. Prasanna, Bedi, Chandrasekhar ... what do these three bowlers from India have in common?

5. Dog, Fog, Log, ... they are your clues to identifying an Australian bowler, for his surname rhymes with those words. Who is he?

6. Fast bowler Wayne Clark plays for which Australian team ... Western Australia; Queensland; New South Wales; Victoria?

7. Unjumble the letters to make up the name of a West Indian fast bowler ... YNAWE EDINAL.

8. Give the Christian name of each of the following West Indian bowlers ... Roberts, Phillips, Holding.

9. Fill in the missing letters to name a New Zealand bowler ... R _ C H _ _ _   _ O _ L _ N G _ .

10. Bowler Joel Garner has played for the West Indies XI in a World Series cricket match ... true or false?

Hidden in the circle below is the mixed-up name of a famous Pakistan bowler who also plays for North-amptonshire. The first letter is 'S' . . . now see if you can work out the name!

WICKET-KEEPERS

Wicket-keeping is an art in itself. There have been some spectacular performers behind the stumps in the history of the game. Flamboyant. Often brilliant batsmen. Will these questions stump YOU?

1. The most dismissals ever by a wicket-keeper in one innings is eight. True or False?

2. Arnold Long of Surrey caught a record number of batsmen in a match against Sussex in 1964. How many?

3. Which wicket-keeper holds the record for the most dismissals in a season?

4. England scored 658–8 declared in an innings against Australia in 1946. What record did wicket-keeper Godfrey Evans set up?

5. Can you name the wicket-keeper who leads the highest wicket-keeper dismissal aggregates in Test Matches?

6. A. E. Dick holds the New Zealand record for most wicket-keeping dismissals in a rubber. How many?

7. Can a wicket-keeper stump a batsman off a no-ball?

8. G. Duckworth was a famous Lancashire wicket-keeper. What great feat did he achieve?

9. Which Middlesex and England wicket-keeper achieved the double of 1025 runs and 104 dismissals in the same season?

10. A well-known cricketer – named G. Boycott! – once stood in as a wicket-keeper in an England Test Match. True or False?

Find the mixed-up wicket-keepers. They're all very well-known.

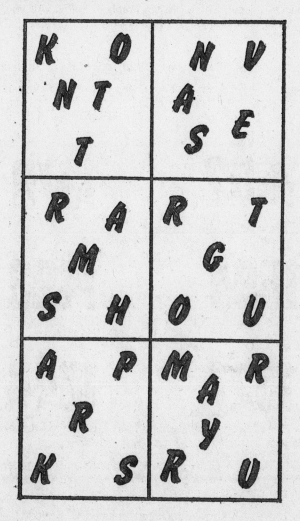

Numbers for a change. John Murray of Middlesex holds the record of most dismissals in a career by a wicket-keeper. There are six numbers below. All you have to do is choose the correct one.

1502   1270

1694   1493

1527   1844

1. A wicket-keeper may place part of his body in front of the wicket when the ball is delivered by the bowler. True or False?

2. Which wicket-keeper removed his pads and got a hat-trick as a bowler in a County Championship match?

3. Who was the first wicket-keeper to make 100 dismissals in John Player League matches?

4. A wicket-keeper catches the ball with one hand and removes the bails with the other to stump a batsman. Would the umpire give him out?

5. Who was known as 'Iron Gloves' when he came to England with a touring side recently?

6. What award did John Murray, the retired Middlesex wicket-keeper, receive in the 1976 New Year's Honours List?

7. D. Lindsay took most catches in a Test Series in 1966/7. For which county and against whom?

8. A wicket-keeper made a record seven dismissals in Britain in 1970, when E. W. Jones played for Glamorgan against Cambridge University. How many catches and how many stumpings?

9. The record for most stumpings in a match is nine. True or False?

10. A. P. E. Knott was once named the Young Cricketer of the Year. But WHICH year was it?

THE COUNTIES

There are seventeen counties in what is now called the Schweppes County Championship. If you're a cricket enthusiast, you're bound to have a favourite county and will know quite a lot about it and its players. But how much do you know about all the others? Here's a mixed bag of questions to get you thinking!

DERBYSHIRE

1. What year was Derbyshire formed? Was it 1870, 1895 or 1908?

2. Can you describe the Derbyshire County badge?

3. What rare feat was achieved by each of the following Derbyshire bowlers: W. H. Copson. H. G. Curgenven and F. C. Brailsford?

4. Can you name the two Derbyshire players who toured Australia and New Zealand in 1974/75?

5. A post-war Derbyshire and England captain was born in Germany. Do you know his name?

6. Who took five wickets with six successive balls for Derbyshire?

7. When did Derbyshire last win the County Championship: 1928, 1936 or 1972?

8. Who was the captain of the County at the start of the 1978 season?

9. In 1898, Derbyshire made their highest innings score against Hampshire. What was it?

10. A Derbyshire bowler came fifth in the bowling averages in 1978. What was his name?

Unscramble the letters to find five current Derbyshire players.

IKNDHECR

YORTAL

LRELMI

NNFFCTUELII

INGOTRROBN

ESSEX

In the square we have another jumble of letters. This time two names of Essex players who have played for England are mixed together and we want you to unscramble them. To start off, one begins with 'L' and the other with 'D'.

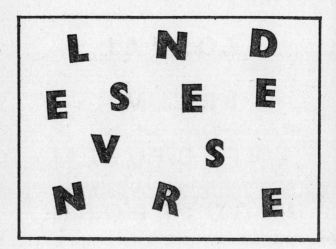

1. In what year was the club formed? (It was before 1880.)

2. Can you describe the Essex badge?

3. Who is the current captain?

4. An Essex player won a World Cup winners' soccer medal in 1966. Do you know his name?

5. Playing against the Australians in 1975, Robin Hobbs scored the fastest century in first-class cricket for 55 years. How long did it take him?

6. Have Essex ever won the County Championship?

7. Essex made a lowest-ever innings score of 30 in 1901. Were they playing against: Kent, Leicestershire or Yorkshire?

8. Who captained Essex immediately before Trevor Bailey? He's still a well-known name in cricket.

9. Last season, Essex reached the semi-finals of the Gillette Cup. True or False?

10. Can you name the Essex batsman who finished highest in the 1978 cricket averages?

GLAMORGAN

1. Name the only Glamorgan player to have captained England.

2. How many times have Glamorgan been County Champions?

3. Can you describe the County badge?

4. When was the club formed?

5. Who was the captain of Glamorgan in 1978?

6. In 1951, Glamorgan scored more than 500 runs in an innings against Derbyshire at Cardiff. What was the exact score?

7. A player in the current side has scored more runs than any other Glamorgan player. Who is he?

8. A record first-wicket stand took place in 1972 for Glamorgan against Northamptonshire. Do you know the score?

9. Which Glamorgan bowler conceded 36 runs off six successive balls in 1968?

10. Only one Glamorgan player has scored a century and taken a hat-trick in the same match. Can you name him?

Below is perhaps the most famous Glamorgan name in cricket. He served the County as player, captain and secretary for nearly forty years before retiring in 1977. Fill in the missing blanks to discover his identity.

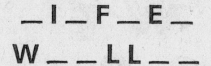

_ I _ F _ E _

W _ _ L L _ _

GLOUCESTERSHIRE

Another famous cricket name is hidden in the circle on this page. Just to make it a little more difficult, we've spelt his name twice, so there are two of everything! He was a batsman and he played for Gloucestershire.

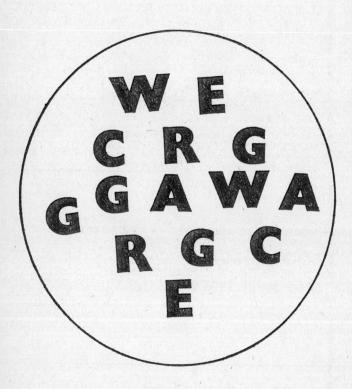

1. What are the Gloucestershire County Club colours?

2. Who hit the stumps five times with consecutive balls against Yorkshire in 1922?

3. Who is the captain of the County and where does he come from?

4. He succeeded another famous name who had led the County for eight years. Who was this former captain?

5. How many times have Gloucestershire won the County Championship?

6. Have they ever won the Gillette Cup?

7. One particular player holds every single batting record for Gloucestershire, scoring 33,664 in his career which included 113 hundreds. Can you name him?

8. Which Gloucestershire player was the first wicket-keeper to stump all three victims of a hat-trick in a first-class match?

9. Who scored a century and did the hat-trick for Gloucestershire against Essex in 1972?

10. How many catches did Wally Hammond hold in first-class matches in the 1928 season? 49, 78 or 98?

HAMPSHIRE

1. The Hampshire Cricket Club was formed in: 1877, 1869, 1863?

2. All the Hampshire honours have come in recent years. First, how many times have they won the County Championship?

3. How many times have they won the Gillette Cup?

4. They have never won the Benson and Hedges Cup. Is this statement true or false?

5. Can you describe the Hampshire County badge?

6. Derek Shackleton was supreme as a bowler for Hampshire. In how many consecutive seasons did he take 100 first-class wickets?

7. And how many wickets did he take for Hampshire during his career which spanned 1948–1969: 2,183; 2,946; 2,669?

8. Two Hampshire all-rounders scored 10,000 runs and took 1,000 wickets in first-class careers before 1939. Can you name them? (To help you, their initials were A. S. and J. A.)

9. Barry Richards has scored many brilliant centuries for the County. But do you know where he was born?

10. Only one cricketer played for Hampshire in both their Championship-winning sides. Who was he?

The players below all represent Hampshire . . . but only one of the three was born in England. Do you know which one?

B. A RICHARDS	
C. G. GREENIDGE	
R. M. C. GILLIAT	

KENT

Kent have been quite a successful cricket club, with a fair share of honours. Let's start with a numbers question. They did NOT win a trophy in one of the years below. Can you say which one?

1906	
1913	
1967	
1970	
1972	
1973	
1975	

1. When was the Club formed?

2. Name the club colours.

3. Now describe the club badge, please.

4. Kent have won the County Championship on eight occasions. Would you say that is correct?

5. Who is the captain of Kent?

6. Kent won the Schweppes County Championship in 1978. Yes or no?

7. One thing is definite. Kent shared the County Championship in 1977 with . . . which County?

8. Kent have been lucky to have two world-class wicket-keepers during the last twenty years. Can you name both of them?

9. A Kentish bowler took most wickets, bowled most overs and most maidens. Who was he?

10. A large tree grows within the playing area of the St Lawrence Ground at Canterbury. What type of tree is it?

LANCASHIRE

1. Every follower of cricket should know the rose of Lancashire. What colour is it — red or white?

2. The present club was formed — when?

3. Many years ago, a batsman named Charles Hallows scored 1,000 runs during the month of May for Lancashire. But in which year?

4. A famous BBC scorer, who died in 1965, was a member of the Lancashire ground staff. Can you name him?

5. Who is the Patron of the Lancashire C.C.C.?

6. And who is the captain of the Club: David Lloyd or Frank Hayes?

7. Lancashire once scored 801 in an innings against Somerset. True or False?

8. J. B. (Brian) Statham was a faithful servant for Lancashire. How many wickets did he take for Lancashire during his 18-year career: 1416, 1816, 2006?

9. Lancashire shared the County Championship title in 1889: but with how many counties?

10. Do you know how many runs were scored for the record second wicket stand by Lancashire?

Find the Lancashire players. To make things easier for a change, we have underlined the first letter of each name. All you need to do is unscramble the letters. One is no longer registered with the county.

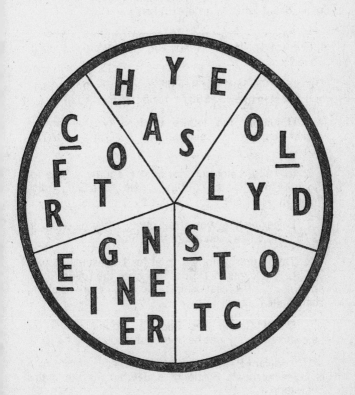

LEICESTERSHIRE

1. Perhaps the greatest all-rounder in English cricket, this Leicestershire player set a record at 20,000 runs and 2,000 wickets in his career, 1906–1939. Fill in the missing letters to give his surname ... WILLIAM _ S _ _ L L .

2. In 1979, Leicestershire celebrates its centenary as a cricket club ... true or false?

3. What is Leicestershire's home ground called ... Grace Road; Majesty Road; Highness Road; Lordship Road?

4. In which year did Ray Illingworth become captain of Leicestershire ... 1967; 1968; 1969; 1970?

5. Unjumble the letters to identify the famous wicket-keeper for Leicestershire ... ORERG RATH-CODL.

6. In 1975, Leicestershire beat a country's side for the first time. Was the country ... New Zealand; India; Pakistan, Australia?

7. Leicestershire won the County Championship in 1975 for the first; second or third time?

8. The highest winning total for Leicestershire was 701 for 4 wickets in 1906. Who were the unlucky opponents ... Worcestershire; Surrey; Warwickshire; Hampshire?

9. David Gower has been a regular player for Leicestershire ... was he born in the county?

10. William Bentley and Mike Turner ... say which is Leicestershire's President and which is the club's Secretary.

Our artist has altered this drawing of Leicestershire's club badge, so there's something missing . . . what is it?

MIDDLESEX

Which of the three sketches below is the correct Middlesex club badge?

1. Lord's is well known as Middlesex's ground. In which area of London is it based . . . Putney; Highgate; St John's Wood or Chelsea?

2. J. D. Robertson achieved the highest individual batting score of a Middlesex player in 1949, playing against Worcestershire. Did he get . . . 321; 331; 381?

3. Only one of these players is a Middlesex team member . . . Phil Slocombe; Javed Miandad; Clive Rice; Mike Gatting; Graham Roope. Which one?

4. Denis Compton was an all-time great batsman, who played for Middlesex throughout his cricket career, between the years . . . 1936 until 1950; 1957; 1961 or 1964?

5. J. M. Brearley is the Middlesex captain. Give both his Christian names.

6. All these Middlesex players have played for England in Test Matches . . . Barlow; Selvey; Radley; Edmonds; Emburey. True or false?

7. Unjumble the letters to give the surname of the Middlesex wicket-keeper . . . LOGUD.

8. Fill in the missing letters to identify Middlesex's West Indian fast bowler . . . _ A Y _ _   D _ _ I E _.

9. One of the fastest scores in cricket history was made by C. I. J. Smith of Middlesex, in 1938, when he got 69 runs in . . . how many minutes? 15; 20; 25; 30; 35; 40 minutes?

10. The County Championship has been won outright 6 times by Middlesex. When was the last time they won it . . . outright . . . 1959; 1963; 1971; 1976; 1978?

6

NORTHAMPTONSHIRE

1. In which year did Northamptonshire join the county championship . . . 1895; 1900; 1905 or 1910?

2. R. Subba Row achieved the highest individual batting score for Northamptonshire in 1958. Is that county record . . . 250; 300; 350 or 400 runs?

3. In 1914, G. J. Thompson got an unusual hat-trick of wickets . . . were they all stumped; all caught; all LBW?

4. Name the captain who led Northamptonshire to victory in the 1976 Gillette Cup.

5. Who was the bowler, and at the time, captain of India, who left Northamptonshire in 1977 to play for Kerry Packer? Unjumble the letters . . . SENHIB IDBE.

6. During the 1932 season, V. W. Jupp took a remarkable number of wickets off Kent in an innings . . . 8, 9, or 10 wickets?

7. In which town is the Northamptonshire cricket club based . . . Kettering; Northampton; Wellingborough?

8. Fill in the missing letters to identify the Pakistani who has got lots of wickets for Northamptonshire. _ _ R F _ _ Z N _ W A _.

9. Northamptonshire batsman David Steele played for England in 1977 . . . true or false?

10. Playing against Warwickshire in 1965, Northamptonshire wicket-keeper L. A. Johnson made 10 dismissals in the match, by . . . 5 caught and 5 stumped or 3 caught and 7 stumped, or all 10 caught, or 8 caught and 2 stumped?

Which one of the three sketches below is the correct county badge for Northamptonshire?

NOTTINGHAMSHIRE
Fill in the missing letters to give the surnames of seven
Nottinghamshire players.

H _ _ K _ R

_ A Y _ _ R

_ _ R R _ S

H _ S _ A N

J O _ N _ O _

B I _ _ H

W _ L K _ _ S _ N

1. It's a cricket record that a father and son, both playing for Nottinghamshire, each hit a century in the same innings . . . true or false?

2. Former Nottinghamshire captain Gary Sobers amazingly scored 1,000 runs in a season in four countries, which were . . . ?

3. A. K. Walker achieved an astounding feat that's never been equalled, when he took a wicket with the last ball of the first innings and took three wickets with his first three balls in the second innings, in a Nottinghamshire versus Leicestershire match. In which year . . . 1936; 1946; 1956 or 1966?

4. Sort out the letters to name this Nottinghamshire player, who because of his entertaining and athletic fielding, is often known as 'the court jester of cricket' . . . KEDRE NADARLL.

5. Nottinghamshire's home, Trent Bridge, is used as a Test Match ground . . . true or false?

6. At a young age, B. French was brought in as a wicket-keeper for Nottinghamshire in the 1977 season. How old was he?

7. Former Nottinghamshire player Doshi bowled left-arm or right-arm?

8. Why was Clive Rice sacked by the club in 1978?

9. Fill in the missing letters to identify this Nottinghamshire captain. _ _ K E _ M _ _ L _ Y .

10. How many times has Nottinghamshire won the County Championship outright . . . 6; 12; 25; or 31 times?

SOMERSET

1. Name the Somerset bowler who took five Australian wickets on his first day of Test Match cricket for England, in 1977.

2. A. W. Wellard scored 31 runs off one over, when Somerset were playing Kent, in which season ... 1911; 1924; 1938 or 1967?

3. During his cricket career from 1909 to 1937, J. C. White set a club record for Somerset taking how many wickets ... 1,356; 2,356 or 3,356?

4. Unjumble the letters to identify this great batsman for Somerset, and also the West Indies ... IVV SIHCADRR.

5. Brian Close retired from playing cricket, as captain of Somerset, in ... 1974; 1975; 1976 or 1977?

6. Harold Gimblett holds the Somerset batting record for ... scoring two separate hundreds in a match; scoring the fastest fifty; scoring the fastest hundred?

7. Fill in the missing letters to name a giant West Indian bowler for Somerset .... _ O _ L G _ _ N _ R .

8. Young Somerset player Brian Rose is a right-handed or left-handed batsman?

9. B. L. Bisgood scored 116 runs playing for Somerset in 1907 ... what was so significant about that?

10. In the 1978 County Championship, Somerset tied with Yorkshire in which position ... 1st, 2nd, 3rd or 4th?

Below, you see three drawings of the Somerset badge
... which one is set at the correct angle?

SURREY

1. An easy question to start with. Name Surrey's famous Test Match ground.

2. When did the county last win the County Championship? Was it in 1971, 1972 or 1974?

3. A Surrey player holds the record for the most wickets taken in any Test Match in the World. He's now a well-known TV commentator. Name him.

4. Which former Surrey player holds the double record of scoring more runs and making more hundreds in first class matches than any other player – Sir Jack Hobbs, Andy Sandham, Peter May or Ken Barrington?

5. Did Surrey first win the Benson and Hedges Cup in 1972, 1974 or 1976?

6. Can you guess the county's highest ever score, achieved against Somerset in 1899? Was it 511, 611 or 811?

7. What unparalleled spell of wicket-taking did Pat Pocock produce in his last two overs against Sussex in 1972? Was it four wickets for seven runs, five wickets for 6 runs, 6 wickets for 5 runs, or seven wickets for four runs?

8. A Surrey wicket-keeper made 12 dismissals for the county in a match against Sussex in 1868 – true or false?

9. Can you say what the last major cricketing honour the county won (up to the end of 1978). Was it the County Championship, the John Player League, the Gillette Cup or the Benson & Hedges Cup?

10. True or false? The county won the County Championship every season from 1952 to 1958.

Can you unjumble the mixed-up names on this page to reveal six cricketers who were all playing for the county in 1977?

NOHJ HIREDC

TAP   KOPCCO

FEOGF DONRLA

MAGRAH ORPEO

BORIN NAMCAKJ

EFOFG ROWTAHH

SUSSEX

1. The Sussex county badge is made up of a number of birds or 'martlets'. How many are depicted on the badge – 4, 6, 8 or 10?

2. Tony Greig scored 156 for the county in his debut championship match. Against which county was the match played – Lancashire, Kent or Yorkshire?

3. Can you say if D. S. Sheppard, who skippered Sussex, was the first county captain to: (a) Be knighted by the Queen. (b) Be made a Bishop. (c) Be made a Lord.

4. In which town is the Sussex county headquarters situated?

5. True or False? Former Sussex and England captain Ted Dexter was born in Milan, Italy.

6. Up to 1978, can you say how many times Sussex have won the County Championship. Is it: (a) 3 times. (b) Twice, or (c) They've never won it?

7. Early Sussex star from 1894 to 1908, C. B. Fry was one of the finest all round sportsmen this country has ever known. He was a fine rugby player, a great athlete and represented England at another sport beside cricket. Can you name that sport? Was it swimming, soccer or table tennis?

8. Sussex have never won the Gillette Cup – true or false?

9. You've all heard of the county's controversial former skipper Tony Greig, but his full initials are A. W. Greig. What name does the 'W' stand for?

10. Why did Sussex sack Tony Greig from the captaincy in 1978?

The person's name (first name and surname) jumbled up in the wicket, visited the Sussex county ground in 1977 and had an historic meeting with Tony Greig in the Captain's Room at the top of the pavilion. The whole world of cricket was never the same again. Name this person.

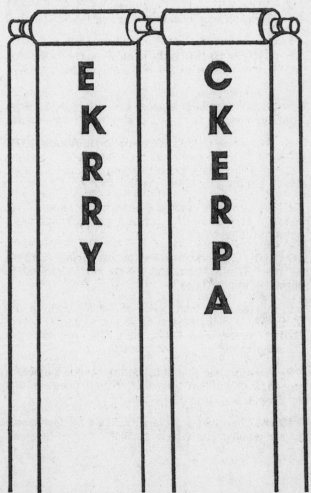

E
K
R
R
Y

C
K
E
R
P
A

WARWICKSHIRE

1. Warwickshire's Mike (M. J. K.) Smith won 50 cricket caps for England and also represented his county at another sport in 1956. Was that sport, soccer, rugby union or hockey?

2. Up to 1978, can you say when the county last won the County Championship? Was it in 1960, 1970 or 1972?

3. SNDIEN SAISM is the jumbled up name of which well-known Warwickshire and England batsman?

4. True or False? Jim Stewart hit 17 sixes in Warwickshire's match against Lancashire in 1959 to establish a record for the most sixes in a single match.

5. In a match against Warwickshire in August 1977, Chris Old made the second fastest century in the history of first class cricket, taking only 37 minutes. Which county was Chris playing for?

6. Warwickshire's home ground is the famous Test venue of Edgbaston. But can you say on which city's outskirts does it lie?

7. In the England squad that played against Australia on the 1978–79 tour, there were no Warwickshire players – true or false?

8. Warwickshire can boast of fielding four of the best West Indies players of recent years – Gibbs, Kanhai, Murray and Kallicharran. Can you give the Christian names of two of those stars?

9. Warwickshire's famous county badge depicts a ragged staff and an animal. Can you guess if that animal is a lion, a bird or a bear?

10. 887 and 657 are Warwickshire's highest scores for and against. But which is which?

11. The diagram depicted on this page is a plan of Warwickshire's home ground – or is it? Answer 'yes' or 'no'.

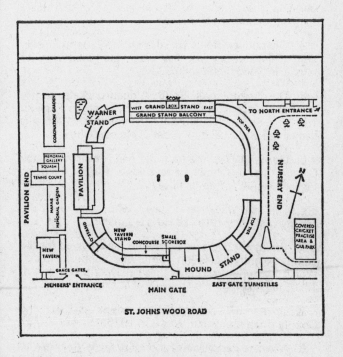

WORCESTERSHIRE

1. True or false? Tom Graveney was the last player from the county to skipper England.

2. You'll have to make a guess at the answer to this question, but I'm sure you'll agree it's rather unusual! In 1889, a strange thing happened when the groundsman resowed bare patches on the Worcester ground. Can you guess what emerged instead of grass? Was it spinach, cabbage or turnips?

3. The county didn't win the County Championship until 1964, but can you say when they next won it? Was it in 1965, 1969 or 1970?

4. The first coloured South African cricketer to rise to county cricket in England and become an England Test player made his debut for the county in 1965. His names are Basil Lewis — what is his surname?

5. Up to 1978, the county had never won the Gillette Cup, the Benson and Hedges Cup or the John Player League — true or false?

6. Can you name the player who took over the county captaincy in 1971? He is Norman _ _ _ _ _ _ _

7. Two great overseas stars who have played for the county recently are Glenn Turner and Vanburn Holder. Which two countries have these players taken part in Test Matches for?

8. Up to 1978, when did the county last win the County Championship? Was it in 1976, 1974 or 1973?

9. A Worcester player of the 1930s was the Nawab of Pataudi who became one of the few players to play Tests for two countries. Can you name one of those countries?

10. On the Worcestershire county badge, an item of fruit is depicted three times. Is that fruit: an apple, a pear or an orange?

How about this for an unusual picture to find in a cricket book! Can you say which Worcestershire player made many appearances in goal for this soccer club? Was it Ted Hemsley, Doug Inchmore, Jim Cumbes or J. A. Ormrod?

YORKSHIRE

The highest individual total scored against the county was by the legendary Dr. W. G. Grace, who in 1876 scored 318 not out. Now see if you can answer the following 11 questions correctly.

1. One of Yorkshire's and England's greatest opening batsmen died in January 1978 aged 83. His surname was Sutcliffe. Can you give his Christian name?

2. Can you guess in which year I made my debut for the county? Was it in 1962, 1964 or 1966?

3. Yorkshire have won the County Championship more times than any other county. True or false?

4. No player has ever captained Yorkshire who hasn't been born in the county. True or false?

5. Wilfred Rhodes was a famous Yorkshire player. Can you guess how many times he did the 'double' of 1,000 runs and 100 wickets in a season? Was it 5 times, 12 times or 16 times?

6. In the 'wars of the roses' with Lancashire, is Yorkshire the white rose or the red rose?

7. What unique 'double' did Yorkshire's George Hirst achieve in 1906? Was it: (a) 2,000 runs and 200 wickets in a season. (b) 3,000 runs and 300 wickets in a season. (c) 200 catches in a season?

8. On May 20th, 1965, the county made their lowest score ever, in a match against Hampshire. Can you guess if that score was 18, 23, 25 or 27?

9. One of the greatest fast bowlers of all time made his debut for the county in 1949. He began his Test career by taking 29 wickets in 4 Tests and with his 'fiery' fast bowling he became the first player to capture over 300 wickets in Test cricket. Can you name him?

10. True or false? Yorkshire lost only 3 county matches in the four seasons 1925–28.

11. Here's a really tough question. Of all the dates shown on this page, Yorkshire failed to win the County Championship on only one occasion! Which is the odd date out?

**1922 1923 1924
1925 1926 1931
1932 1933 1935
1937 1938 1939**

7.

RECORDS

A great many records have been set in cricket . . . and some of the most important ones are covered here. So if you're 'stumped' by a question, it'll be interesting to look up the answer! This section deals with general cricket.

1. The highest-ever recorded individual score in first-class cricket was achieved by Hanif Mohammad, in 1959, during a Karachi v. Bahawalpur match at Karachi, Pakistan. Exactly how many runs were scored – 399, 499 or 599?

2. In 1947, Denis Compton set a record for most runs scored in one season, and it's still unbeaten. Did he score a total of 1,816; 2,816 or 3,816 runs?

3. It was back in 1920 when the fastest hundred-plus was scored by P. G. H. Fender, in a Surrey v. Northants match. He scored 100 runs, in how many minutes – 25, 30 or 35?

4. The best record for 'most wickets taken in a match' occurred in 1956, when England were playing Australia at Manchester. No less than 19 wickets were taken for only 90 runs! Who was the bowler?

5. In the history of cricket, only one bowler has ever achieved the 'double' of getting 2,000 runs and 200 wickets in a season, in 1906. Name the bowler.

6. The world record for throwing the cricket ball (not while playing, of course!) has remained at 140 yards 2 feet since 1884! True or false?

7. Retired in 1975, J. T. Murray holds the record for most dismissals in a career by a wicket-keeper. What were his number of dismissals . . . 1,128; 1,372; 1,527; 1,725?

8. Excluding wicket-keepers, F. E. Woolley made the most catches in a career. How many . . . 840; 1,015; 1,533; 2,002?

9. The highest total of runs of two competing sides amounted when Victoria played New South Wales in 1927. How many runs . . . 1,001; 1,107; 1,149; 1,171?

10. The highest number of runs ever scored by a county in first-class cricket is 887. It happened almost a hundred years ago, in 1896! Which was the county – Yorkshire; Somerset; Sussex; Lancashire or Glamorgan?

Now what about the world record for the lowest total of runs by one side in a match? It took place, in 1959–60, between the sides of Border and Natal, in East London, South Africa. How many runs did Border score in their first innings? . . . 34; 37; 58; 93; 102?

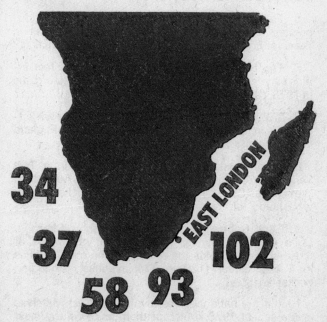

1. Do you know which player has scored the most runs – 7,624 – for England in Test Match cricket? It's one of these four . . . Peter May; Ray Illingworth; Tony Greig; Colin Cowdrey?

2. For a Test debut, R. E. Foster scored the most runs in an England v. Australia match in 1904. What was his record score . . . 107; 152; 190; 223; 287?

3. The fastest Test century was scored by J. M. Gregory in 1922 when Australia met South Africa in Johannesburg. In how many minutes . . . 100; 92; 86; 70?

4. The slowest individual batting in a Test Match was by J. T. Murray playing for England against Australia in 1963. In 100 minutes, he scored no more than how many runs . . . 13; 9; 3; 1; 0?

5. Freddie Trueman was one of the all-time great bowlers, and set a record for the most wickets taken in Tests for England. 141; 189; 236; 307 or 511 wickets?

6. The best figures for wickets taken in a Test innings by Ian Botham, in an England v. Pakistan game in 1978, came to . . . 6, 7, 8, 9 or 10 wickets for 34 runs?

7. 252 is the record number of dismissals for wicket-keeping in a Test career. Name the famous England wicket-keeper who achieved this.

8. Most dismissals by a wicket-keeper in a Test Series was 26. This happened in the 1975–76 Australia v. West Indies Series. Name the Australian wicket-keeper who holds this record.

9. Gary Sobers; Ian Chappell; Bobby Simpson, Colin Cowdrey; Walter Hammond . . . which one of those cricketers holds the record for the most catches in a Test career (120 in 114 matches), excluding wicket-keepers?

10. Of the national sides involved in Test Matches, at the end of 1978, which of them has won the most matches (199) . . . England; Australia; South Africa; West Indies; New Zealand; India or Pakistan?

Below is a circle containing the jumbled letters of the full name of the Englishman who has made the most appearances in Test Matches for England. Put the letters together correctly and you'll know who the cricketer is.

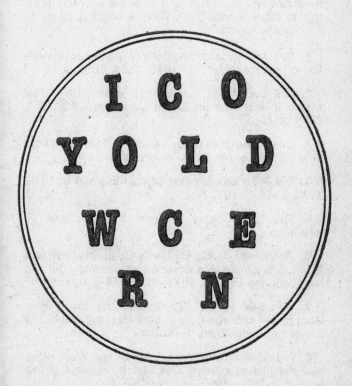

DATES

It's always difficult to put a date to an event, so these questions will really test your knowledge of the game. But to make it easier, a choice of dates is given for most of the questions.

1. Can you say when the County Championship was first played for? Was it in 1840, 1864, 1890 or 1901?

2. Jim Laker took a record 19 wickets in a Test Match against Australia. Did it happen in 1950, 1954, 1956 or 1958?

3. One of the greatest cricketers of all time was born in 1848 and died in 1915. Who was he?

4. Did Mike Brearley first captain England in 1974, 1975, 1976 or 1977?

5. The 1970 County Championship was won by which county?

6. At the age of 42, England's Colin Cowdrey was flown to Australia as a replacement batsman. Did this happen in the 1972–3, 1973–4 or 1974–5 Test series?

7. Was it in 1973, 1975 or 1977 that the brilliant West Indian cricketer Gary Sobers was knighted by the Queen in Bridgetown, Barbados?

8. A Test Match between Australia and West Indies saw the first-ever tie in Test Match cricket. Did this happen in 1940, 1950, 1960 or 1970?

9. When did England first play one day international matches for the Prudential Trophy – 1970, 1972 or 1974?

10. In this year, Tony Greig joined Kerry Packer's cricket 'circus' and was sacked from the England captaincy. Was that year 1975, 1976 or 1977?

11. Starting at the top of the circle and working clockwise, can you take one letter from each segment in turn to spell a nine-letter county that won the County Championship for the first time in 1948?

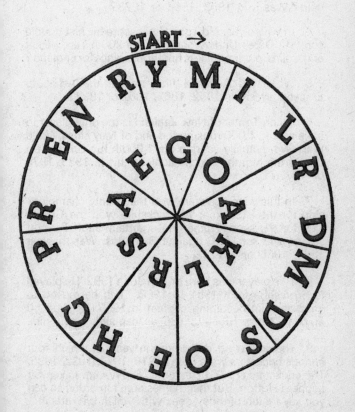

1. When was the County Championship title last shared before 1977? 1948, 1950 1961?

2. Which major major cricketing country was banished from the Test Match scene for political reasons in 1970?

3. When was the first women's cricket World Cup held? Was it in 1953, 1963 or 1973?

4. In which year did Tony Greig score his first double century; Derek Underwood take his 200th Test wicket and Colin Cowdrey make a final appearance for England?

5. When did Australia first present the Ashes to England. Was it in 1852, 1862, 1882 or 1892?

6. Glenn Turner of New Zealand is the only player to have scored 1,000 runs by the end of May since World War Two, actually scoring his 1,000th run on the last day of the month! Did he achieve this in 1973, 1975 or 1977?

7. In this year, Yorkshire won the county championship for the 31st time, Warwickshire won the Gillette Cup for the second time and a certain Geoff Boycott scored 243 for MCC against Barbados. Was the year 1960, 1968 or 1972?

8. This player was born on 8th June 1932. He played for Yorkshire from 1951 to 1968. Then he moved to Leicestershire becoming captain in 1969. He won 66 England caps, 1958–73 (36 as captain). Name him.

9. The following dates are the years in which four famous cricketers were born: 1916, 1872, 1922, 1935. The cricketers are Ted Dexter, C. B. Fry, Jim Laker, Sir Leonard Hutton. But their names aren't in order, so can you say which birthday goes with which cricketer?

10. In a Test Match between England and Pakistan at Edgbaston in 1962, play was held up for a few minutes because of the appearance of a creature on the pitch. Was that creature a dog, a cat or a mouse?

Kent has won the County Championship on two of the dates shown in the six panels. Put a cross next to the two dates you think are the correct ones.

1912	
1913	
1920	
1940	
1960	
1970	

RULES

Cricket can be a complex game — especially if you don't know the rules! Try and answer these questions: if you happen to fail with some of them, at least you'll learn something!

1. Eight-ball overs were once used as an experiment in first-class cricket. In what year?

2. A batsman can be stumped off a wide. Yes or No?

3. How does an umpire signal a 'dead ball' to the scorers?

4. The bowler delivers the ball, the umpire calls 'wide' — but the batsman hits the ball. What happens?

5. The height of the stumps should be: (a) 28 inches (b) 29 inches (c) 30 inches?

6. When the two captains toss a coin for choice of innings, the away captain calls. But the toss must be made not less than how many minutes before start of play?

7. A substitute comes on as a runner for an injured batsman. Does this move need the consent of the opposing captain?

8. The umpire raises both hands above his head. What is he signalling?

9. Is a bowler allowed a trial run-up before he bowls?

10. A pitch is 22 yards long, but how WIDE should it be?

There are nine ways that a batsman can be out. Fill in as many as you can in the blanks below.

1._____

2._____

3._____

4._____

5._____

6._____

7._____

8._____

9._____

The positions on the cricket field are both strangely named and strangely placed . . . if one has no knowledge of the game. Below are the letters A to D. If a right-handed batsman is at the top wicket, what positions would they represent?

C

• • •
•
BATSMAN   D

B

• • •

A

1. The ball raps the batsman on the wrist and is caught by a fielder. Is he out?

2. A bat should not be longer than … how many inches?

3. Now one with a difference. A batsman slams the ball straight out of the ground and it is lost. What will the umpire do?

4. One bail is knocked off. Is the batsman out?

5. Who makes the Laws of Cricket? (a) Test and County Cricket Board (b) Wisdens Cricketers' Almanack (c) MCC

6. Another tricky one. A batsman throws his cap at the ball to stop it going over the boundary. The umpire orders the ball to be bowled again. Is he correct?

7. LBW is another difficult law. The ball pitches outside the batsman's leg stump and hits his leg in front of the wicket. Out or not?

8. The ball is a very important part of the game, obviously. Do you know how much it weighs? Not more than (a) $5\frac{3}{4}$ ozs (b) $6\frac{1}{4}$ ozs (c) 6 ozs.

9. Is it possible for a cricket match to be played without bails on the stumps?

10. Final question. The ball knocks off a bail. It lodges between the stumps and does not reach the ground. What does the umpire decide?

How observant are you? Here are some of my popular instructional strips. At first glance, they may appear to be exactly the same, but in each case, six changes have been made to the second strip. Can you spot those changes?

Geoff Boycott on Cricket

PLAY YOURSELF IN

I KEEP MY SCORE TICKING OVER WITH SINGLES UNTIL I FEEL CONFIDENT TO PLAY MY SHOTS

ALWAYS HIT THE BAD BALL, BUT WAIT UNTIL TO THE LIGHT, THE BOWLER'S ACTION AND THE PACE OF THE BALL OFF THE PITCH BEFORE YOU START PLAYING ALL SHOTS

SOMETIMES BATSMEN GET OUT BECAUSE THEY TRY TO PLAY TOO MANY SHOTS AT THE BEGINNING OF THEIR INNINGS. THEY DO NOT GIVE THEMSELVES TIME TO GET USED TO THE CONDITIONS 'IN THE MIDDLE'.

Geoff Boycott on Cricket

CHOOSING YOUR OWN BAT

MANY CRICKETERS ASK ME HOW TO CHOOSE A BAT. MY ADVICE IS TO TAKE GREAT CARE IN SELECTING YOUR BAT FOR 'FEEL' AND BALANCE.

I CHOOSE MY BAT BY PICKING IT UP AND PLAYING A FEW 'FRESH AIR' SHOTS UNTIL I FIND ONE WHICH 'PICKS UP' EASILY AND I FEEL HAPPY WITH. A WELL BALANCED BAT SHOULD LIFT EASILY AND FEEL AN EXTENSION OF YOUR LEFT ARM.

REMEMBER NO ONE ELSE CAN CHOOSE YOUR BAT FOR YOU — ONLY THE ONE WHICH YOU 'FEEL' IS RIGHT.

Geoff Boycott on Cricket

CHOOSING YOUR OWN BAT

MANY CRICKETERS ASK ME HOW TO CHOOSE A BAT. MY ADVICE IS TO TAKE GREAT CARE IN SELECTING YOUR BAT FOR FEEL AND BALANCE.

I CHOOSE MY BAT BY PICKING IT UP AND PLAYING A FEW 'FRESH AIR' SHOTS UNTIL I FIND ONE WHICH 'PICKS UP' EASILY AND I FEEL HAPPY WITH. A WELL BALANCED BAT SHOULD LIFT EASILY AND FEEL AN EXTENSION OF YOUR LEFT ARM.

REMEMBER NO ONE ELSE CAN CHOOSE YOUR BAT FOR YOU— BUY THE ONE WHICH YOU 'FEEL' IS RIGHT.

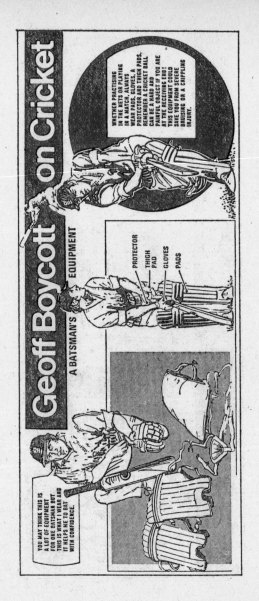

Geoff Boycott on Cricket

A BATSMAN'S EQUIPMENT

WHETHER PRACTISING IN THE NETS OR PLAYING IN A MATCH, ALWAYS WEAR PADS, GLOVES, A PROTECTOR AND THIGH PADS. REMEMBER A CRICKET BALL CAN BE A VERY HARD AND PAINFUL OBJECT IF YOU ARE AT THE RECEIVING END! THIS EQUIPMENT COULD SAVE YOU FROM SEVERE BRUISING OR A CRIPPLING INJURY.

PROTECTOR
THIGH PAD
GLOVES
PADS

YOU MAY THINK THIS IS A LOT OF EQUIPMENT FOR ONE BATSMAN BUT THIS IS WHAT I WEAR AND IT HELPS ME TO BAT WITH CONFIDENCE.

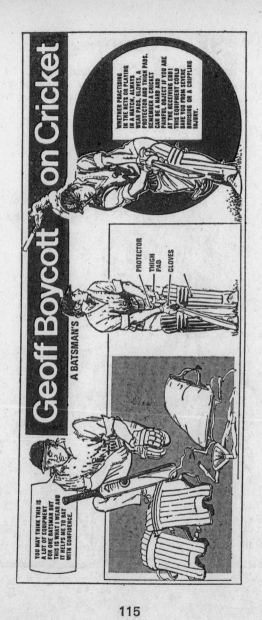

Geoff Boycott on Cricket

A BATSMAN'S

PROTECTOR
THIGH PAD
GLOVES

YOU MAY THINK THIS IS A LOT OF EQUIPMENT FOR ONE BATSMAN BUT THIS IS WHAT I WEAR AND IT HELPS ME TO BAT WITH CONFIDENCE.

WHETHER PRACTISING IN THE NETS OR PLAYING IN A MATCH, ALWAYS WEAR PADS, GLOVES, A PROTECTOR AND THIGH PADS. REMEMBER A CRICKET CAN BE A HARD AND PAINFUL OBJECT IF YOU ARE AT THE RECEIVING END! THIS EQUIPMENT COULD SAVE YOU FROM SEVERE BRUISING OR A CRIPPLING INJURY.

MY SECTION

This is the Geoff Boycott Cricket Quiz Book, so I think it's only fair that I should ask you a few questions about me! On this and the following pages are a few that should have you scratching your heads!

1. When was I born?

2. And where was I born?

3. Which school did I attend?

4. When did I make my debut in cricket for York-shire?

5. I was awarded my county cap in 1964. Or was I? Can you give me the correct answer?

6. I scored 243 for the MCC. Can you say when and against whom?

7. Have I ever been elected Young Cricketer of the Year?

8. I achieved something I was very proud of in 1977, in front of my own Headingly crowd against the Australians. What was it?

9. I played 25 innings in first-class cricket in 1978. Do you know how many runs I scored? Was it (a) 1,596 (b) 1,233 (c) 1,644?

10. I made the highest individual innings score for Yorkshire in the Gillette Cup (146) and the Benson and Hedges Cup (102). Against which counties?

Choose the first season I was appointed County captain of Yorkshire.

1969	
1970	
1971	
1972	
1973	

1. With a lot of dedication – and a certain amount of good fortune – I completed 30,000 runs in first-class cricket. In which year?

2. What is my highest score ever in this country?

3. And what is the highest score I've made in Test cricket?

4. I don't bowl very often, but when I do, what is my style?

5. In fact, I had a real flourish with the ball in a Test Match back in 1964. Do you know what my bowling analysis was?

6. I wear contact lenses when I bat. True or False?

7. I was involved in three consecutive first-wicket century partnerships for England. Who was my partner on each occasion?

8. I've been lucky enough to score quite a few hundreds in my career so far . . . but what are the most I've scored in one season?

9. And how many times have I exceeded 1,000 runs in a season?

10. Now we double it! How many times have I scored more than 2,000 runs in a season?

1. Prior to the 1978–79 Aussie tour, how many catches had I made in Test cricket? (I had to look this one up myself!) (a) 20 (b) 25 (c) 34?

2. My name appears in the record books for my part in a 215 partnership for the sixth wicket against Australia in 1977. Who was my partner?

3. In what year did I score my first century for England?

4. I batted on all five days of the Third Test against Australia at Nottingham in 1977. Do you think I am the only player to have done this?

5. In what year was I named Cricketer of the Year by Wisden?

6. Who captained Yorkshire immediately before me?

7. During the England tour of Australia in the winter of 1978–9 I was bothered with a troublesome injury. To what part of my body?

8. And on another tour of Australia and New Zealand in 1970–71, I was forced to return home early. Why?

9. Where did Yorkshire finish in the Schweppes County Championship in 1978?

10. And how many hundreds did I make in the County Championship last season?

I stand third in all-time highest batting averages in an English season. I want you to rearrange, left, the four figures to show the correct amount of runs I've scored, and, right, my correct average.

| 3520 | 120.10 |

SEASON 1978

The 1978 cricket season contained its usual share of thrills, surprises and disappointments for everyone. It wasn't all that long ago, was it – but how many of the happenings do you remember? These questions will tell you!

1. Let's start off simple! First, which county won the Schweppes County Championship?

2. How many points did they score? 292, 288 or 273?

3. Pakistan came to England to play three Test matches. Who won the series?

4. Which county won the Benson and Hedges Cup?

5. England also played two one-day matches in the Prudential Cup in 1978. Against whom, and what were the results?

6. One of Kent's famous England stars did not play for his county at all in 1978. Who was it?

7. Tony Greig – former captain of Sussex and England – has a younger brother Ian who also plays cricket. Both played Sussex League cricket in 1978. For which team?

8. Now some questions about the final first-class cricket averages. Who took most wickets in 1978?

9. How many did he take?

10. Even so, he was not top of the bowling averages. Who was?

Below are three New Zealand cricketers who toured England in 1978. Fill in the gaps to find their names.

_ U R _ _ S _

W _ _ G _ T

E _ _ A R _ _

C _ _ LI _ _ E

Below is a jumbled-up county. Which one is it — and what highly undesirable record did they achieve in 1978?

MHER

INOT

PHTA

NOSR

1. Now some more questions about the final averages for 1978. Only one player exceeded 2,000 runs in the season. Do you know who it was?

2. And a real oddity! Two brothers scored exactly the same amount of runs in 1978, and had exactly the same average. First, who were the brothers?

3. And how many runs did they score: 1,711; 1,171; 1,182?

4. Who was top of the batting averages in 1978?

5. What was his highest score?

6. Who won the Gillette Cup in 1978?

7. Who scored the fastest century of the season?

8. An experimental law regarding the bouncer was recommended last year. What was it?

9. Which county were the John Player League Champions?

10. Four Middlesex men played for England in 1978. How many of them can you name?

1. Six batsmen scored 200 or more in an innings during 1978. How many of them came from overseas?

2. A famous Australian fast bowler retired from Test cricket at the age of 28 last year. Who was he?

3. A Derbyshire player wearing a crash helmet was struck in the face by a ball, which then lodged in his visor. What was the umpire's decision? Did he give the batsman out?

4. In 1978, the Pakistan touring side made a lowest ever score in England. What was it, and against which county?

5. A famous ex-Yorkshire player was named manager of Yorkshire for the following season. Who was he?

6. An England bowler performed a hat-trick on the first day of last season. Who was it?

7. The winners of the Schweppes County Championship in 1978 received prize money of £9,000. True or False?

8. The Australian selectors appointed a surprise captain to their Test XI last year ... But he didn't play against England. Do you know who he was?

9. I captained England in New Zealand last year in three Test matches. What were the results of each?

10. Finally, who headed the catching list in 1978?

Find the batsmen! All were successful during 1978.

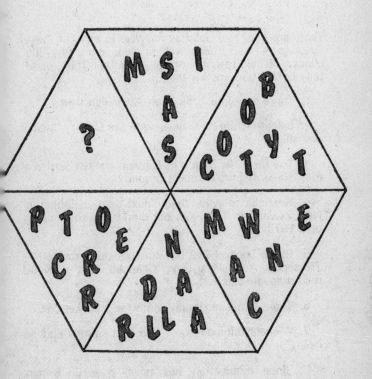

TRUE OR FALSE?

There are only two possible answers to each of these questions – true or false. Which gives you a fifty-fifty chance of being right – or being wrong! Think carefully before you answer them.

1. There are eight balls in an Australian over.

2. Leicestershire have never won the County Championship.

3. The first Test Match in England against Australia took place at Lord's cricket ground.

4. Australia played their 'next-door neighbours' New Zealand in 1945–46, but didn't play them again until 1973!

5. In the Second Test against England in the 1974–75 series, Australia's Greg Chappell took a world record seven catches.

6. There is no maximum width for a cricket bat.

7. Wickets originally only had two stumps and no bails!

8. Since metrication has taken over in Britain, cricket pitches are now 22 metres long instead of 22 yards.

9. Australia won the first women's World Cup competition.

10. To achieve a 'hat-trick', a bowler must take three wickets with consecutive balls in the same over.

11. The badge drawn by our artist below is the Worcestershire county badge.

1. No batsman has ever scored 3,000 runs in a season of County Championship matches.

2. Rohan Kanhai captained India in many Test Matches.

3. Trent Bridge is the Test Match ground situated farthest north in Britain.

4. A batsman cannot be stumped off a no-ball or a wide.

5. The world record distance for a bail being knocked from the wicket by a delivery is over 83 yards!

6. Colin Cowdrey captained England against all six (India, Pakistan, Australia, West Indies, South Africa and New Zealand) Test Match playing countries.

7. As well as appearing in 78 Test Matches for England, Denis Compton also played soccer for Arsenal.

8. W. G. Grace was 60 years of age when he played his last innings of first class cricket in 1908.

9. The top five Minor Counties are allowed to take part in the Gillette Cup competition.

10. Freddie Trueman was the first man to capture over 300 wickets in Test cricket.

1. All the information on this page refers to Surrey County Cricket Club. True or false?

FORMATION OF PRESENT CLUB:
1859

REORGANISED:
1870

COLOURS:
Red and white

BADGE:
White Horse

COUNTY CHAMPIONS:
1906, 1909, 1910, 1913, 1970,
1977 (shared), 1978

GILLETTE CUP WINNERS:
1967, 1974

JOHN PLAYER LEAGUE CHAMPIONS:
1972, 1973, 1976

BENSON & HEDGES CUP WINNERS:
1973, 1976, 1978

1. Essex play their home matches on no fewer than 9 grounds throughout the county!

2. All the following players have represented Pakistan in Test Matches: Younis Ahmed, Asif Iqbal, Wasim Bari, Sunil Gavaskar, Zaheer Abbas.

3. Sir Gary Sobers is the only West Indian cricketer ever to be knighted.

4. In County Cricket, if a bowler delivered two wides and two no balls in an over, then his total number of balls for that over would be ten.

5. The highest number of centuries in a Test Match innings is five by Australia against West Indies in 1954–55.

6. Women cricketers have never played at Lord's.

7. A 'Chinaman' is an unorthodox delivery by a slow right-arm bowler.

8. The maximum number of points a side can score in a County Championship match is 20.

9. The highest individual score in a Test Match is 364 by Len Hutton, (for England v. Australia in 1938).

10. Mike Denness, who captained England, is Scottish.

All the newspaper headlines shown on this page refer to the year 1974. True or false?

HEADINGLEY TEST PITCH SABOTAGED

LEICESTERSHIRE WIN COUNTY CHAMPIONSHIP FOR FIRST TIME

BOB WOOLMER SCORES SLOWEST CENTURY IN HISTORY OF ENGLAND v AUSTRALIA TESTS

BENSON & HEDGES CUP

The one-day cricket game has benefited greatly from this limited-overs competition. How good is your knowledge of the history of the tournament?

1. When was the trophy first played for? 1970, 1971 or 1972?

2. The Benson and Hedges Cup is made of solid gold — true or false?

3. How many teams start off the competition each year — 16, 20 or 24?

4. The teams in the competition include all the county sides plus two teams supplied from the Minor counties and one other team. What is that team?

5. How many overs is each innings limited to in the one day matches?

6. Which county has won the cup three times up to and including 1978?

7. Who were the beaten finalists in 1978?

8. Which county did Mike Proctor lead to victory in the 1977 final?

9. The highest individual score in the competition was by Gordon Greenidge playing for Hampshire against Minor Counties South in 1973. Can you guess if his score was 103, 153, 173 or 203?

10. Up to the end of 1978, no Minor Counties side has ever won a match in the competition — true or false?

In the circle on this page is the jumbled up name of the county who were the first winners of the Benson and Hedges Cup, but all the vowels have been left out of the county's name. Can you say which county it is?

1. Surrey have never won the trophy – true or false?

2. To make way for the competition when it was started, the County Championship three-day programme was reduced from 24 matches to how many?

3. Where is the final traditionally held?

4. The final is played over 60 overs per innings – true or false?

5. The first part of the competition is conducted on a league basis within four groups. How many points are awarded for a win in each match?

6. The first winners of the cup hadn't won a major honour in 90 years of playing first class cricket – true or false?

7. The man of the match award in the 1978 final went to Bob Woolmer who was chosen by the Chairman of the Test selectors. Can you name that Chairman? He is Alec _ _ _ _ _ _ ?

8. Several hat-tricks have been achieved in the competition, but only one in a final. Ken Higgs did it in 1974 against Surrey. For which county was Ken playing – Leicestershire, Kent or Yorkshire?

9. Can you guess the winning margin in the 1978 final? Was it: 6 wickets, 7 wickets, 45 runs or 60 runs?

10. The two skippers in the 1978 final were Eddie Barlow and Alan Ealham. Which one of them eventually held up the trophy?

Now you've answered the questions on the Benson and Hedges Cup, study the picture on this page, then say if this is a picture of the trophy awarded to the winners of this competition. Answer 'yes' or 'no'.

DON'T MISS THE
GEOFF BOYCOTT
CRICKET ANNUAL!

Cricket fans everywhere will be delighted to know that this year Geoff Boycott is presenting his own cricket annual. It's a real cricketing souvenir . . . 96 pages packed with the very best photographs of the exciting world of cricket, taken by Patrick Eagar, the world's top cricket photographer. The annual is on sale at the beginning of September.

ORDER YOUR COPY NOW!

On this and the next few pages, you'll find an artist's impressions of a number of top cricketers. From the brief clues provided, how many can you recognise?

This Aussie fast bowler partnered Dennis Lillee to create havoc among the England batsmen in more than one series.

Chris Old (right) and the other player helped to bowl out India for 42, at Lord's in 1974. Who is he?

This Kent spin bowler once took 8 wickets for 9 runs against Sussex. Name him I

This is Barry _ _ _ _ , a Lancashire batsman who has played for England.

An Aussie wicket-keeper, now with Kerry Packer.
Can you identify him?

No clues for identifying this wicket-keeper. He's world-famous!

GEOFF BOYCOTT
WRITES FOR
TIGER

Once again this summer, TIGER ... the top sports paper
... is planning to print a great series of cricket articles
written by Geoff Boycott, the man who is always in the
news! Last year's series was hailed as a real winner ...
and the new series promises to be even better. Get a
copy of TIGER today and get up to date with a whole
new world of sporting adventure ... it's top of the
league for sport!

ORDER YOUR COPY NOW—AT THE PAPER SHOP!

ANSWERS

The Schweppes County Championship
Page 8
1. 1864 2. Nottinghamshire and Gloucestershire 3. Kent 4. K. G. Suttle 5. Surrey 6. 1977 7. Middlesex and Kent 8. .887 9. No 10. Yorkshire, Surrey, Kent, Lancashire.

Page 9
Close, Compton, Cowdrey, Botham, Denness, Trueman.

Page 10
Fred Trueman.

Page 11
1. H. Verity, Yorkshire 2. Bob Willis 3. Jack Hobbs 4. Surrey 5. 1952–1958 6. Northamptonshire 7. A. E. Fagg 8. 555. H. Sutcliffe and P. Holmes of Yorkshire 9. 1968 10. D. S. Sheppard.

Page 12
1. Nottinghamshire, Lancashire, Surrey 2. Nine 3. Surrey 4. Essex, Northamptonshire, Somerset, Sussex 5. Glamorgan 6. Warwickshire 7. 1960 8. Warwickshire 9. 1975 10. Denis Compton and Bill Edrich.

Page 13
Lord's (Middlesex), The Oval (Surrey), Trent Bridge (Nottinghamshire), Old Trafford (Lancashire), Edgbaston (Warwickshire), Headingley (Yorkshire).

John Player League
Page 14
1. 1969 2. Lancashire 3. Kent 4. 3 times 5. Essex 6. Hampshire 7. Gilliat 8. Trophy 9. Middlesex, Yorkshire 10. Somerset, Gloucestershire.

Page 15
Middlesex.

Page 16
4 wickets in 4 balls.

Page 17
1. 4 points 2. 2 points 3. 40 overs 4. Viv Richards
5. 115 6. It was the shortest John Player League
match 7. 814 8. Kent beat Northamptonshire 9.
Somerset 10. False.

The Gillette Cup

Page 18
1. Lord's 2. 60 3. Sussex 4. 1977 5. Lancashire
1970-2 6. C. G. Greenidge 177 7. He took four
wickets in five balls 8. Three 9. Middlesex, Cam-
bridgeshire, Shropshire 10. False. It was Sussex.

Page 19
Sussex, Yorkshire, Kent, Gloucestershire.

Page 20
Lloyd.

Page 21
1. (a) 2. (a) 3. (b) 4. (a) 5. (b) 6. (a) 7. (b)
8. (b) 9. (a) 10. (b).

Tests v. India

Page 22
1. 1932 2. Six 3. 42 4. (d) 5. Chandrasekhar 6.
(a) 7. True 8. J. M. Patel 9. None 10. V. Mankad,
P. R. Umrigar.

Page 23
Bedi, Roy, Engineer.

Page 24
Lahore and Karachi are in Pakistan!

Page 25
1. True 2. Vinoo Mankad 3. 1971 4. A. L. Wadekar
5. S. M. Gavaskar 6. Colin Cowdrey 7. Bombay 8.
Fifteen 9. True 10. Nine.

Tests v. Pakistan

Page 26
1. Mohammad   2. Asif Iqbal, Intikhab Alam   3. Intikhab Alam   4. (a)   5. Eight   6. Captain of first Pakistan touring side of England, 1954   7. D. C. S. Compton   8. Yes. Hanif Mohammad, 1961   9. K. F. Barrington, M. C. Cowdrey   10. (b).

Page 27
Underwood.

Page 28
Amiss, Cowdrey, Pullar, Graveney, Dexter, Compton.

Page 29
1. Mushtaq Mohammad   2. Bahawalpur, Hyderabad, Karachi, Lahore, Peshawar, Rawalpindi   3. True   4. 87   5. 2nd wicket partnership of 248   6. D. L. Underwood   7. 1274 for 25 wkts   8. E. R. Dexter   9. Highest 3rd wkt. stand in cricket   10. True.

Tests v. West Indies

Page 30
1. 1928   2. 849   3. Jamaica   4. 1963, 1966, 1969, 1973   5. West Indies won all three   6. The Oval   7. A. W. Greig   8. West Indies   9. The Wisden Trophy   10. Hampshire.

Page 31
Boyce.

Page 32
Bridgetown, Georgetown, Kingston, Port of Spain.

Page 33
1. Lancashire   2. Brian Close   3. True   4. Derek Randall   5. Nottinghamshire   6. 10   7. David Steele   8. 98   9. 71   10. Ray Illingworth.

Tests v. Australia

Page 34
1. 1882   2. D. K. Lillee   3. I. M. Chappell   4. D. G. Bradman   5. 380   6. 214 minutes   7. Massie   8. 19 for 90   9. 1902   10. R. E. Foster.

Page 35
Adelaide, Brisbane, Melbourne, Perth, Sydney.

Page 36
Grace, Yardley, Illingworth, Benaud, Bradman, Chappell, Brearley.

Page 37
1. Yes 2. Slowest 50 in 361 minutes 3. 95 minutes. T. G. Evans 4. England in 1938 5. Innings and 579 runs 6. 364 by Len Hutton in 1938 7. 19 8. 451 runs 9. Yes. Jim Laker 10-53 10. 298.

Page 38
Lillee, Miller, Lindwall, Statham, Trueman, Thomson.

Page 39
1. 7 in 1974 2. 45 3. 191 4. R. G. D. Willis 5. 974 6. 729–6 dec. 7. No 8. False 9. 1970 10. 394 minutes.

Tests v. New Zealand

Page 40
1. 1929–30 2. 53 3. 27 4. 593 runs, 6 wkts 5. 26 runs 6. Dexter 7. Ray Illingworth 8. The first New Zealander to score a century (104 runs) in a Test Match against England 9. B. Sutcliffe 10. New Zealand.

Page 41
Glenn Turner.

Page 42
1. 72 runs 2. Richard – fast, Dayle – medium-pace 3. Chatfield 4. Ian Botham 5. Geoff Howarth 6. False, England won all three matches 7. Bob Taylor 8. Batting 9. Edgar 10. 1st match.

Page 43
Anderson, Bracewell, Wright, Parker.

The World Cup

Page 44
1. England 2. 1975 3. Sri Lanka and East Africa 4. True 5. The Prudential Assurance Company 6. 8 7. G. M. Turner, 171 8. S. Venkataraghavan 9. 60 10. Australia and West Indies.

Page 45
Clive Lloyd.

Page 46
Heading-ley.

Page 47
1. Lord's 2. A run-out 3. Sir Gary Sobers 4. A. W. Greig 5. New Zealand 6. Gary Gilmour 7. 17 runs 8. Clive Lloyd 9. Geoff Boycott 10. West Indies.

Batsmen

Page 48
1. W. G. Grace 2. Jack Hobbs 3. British 4. Cowdrey 5. Pakistan 6. Nottinghamshire 7. Graham Gooch 8. Brearley 9. Greg took over from Ian 10. Bradman.

Page 49
Keith Fletcher.

Page 50
Len Hutton.

Page 51
1. False. The bat must be no more than 38 inches. 2. David Steele 3. Ted Dexter 4. Gordon. Alvin. Rick 5. Gower 6. Bowler 7. Wicket-keeper 8. True 9. Dennis Amiss, because he's the only one to play for Kerry Packer 10. Barrington.

Page 52
Ken McEwan (Essex). Clive Rice (Nottinghamshire). John Hampshire (Yorkshire). Glenn Turner (Worcestershire).

Page 53
I'm playing a square-cut.

Bowlers

Page 54
1. Willis. Bob 2. Derbyshire 3. Geoff Miller 4. Players' Player of the Year 5. Chris Old 6. False 7. Spin 8. 110 9. Right-handed 10. Somerset.

Page 55
R. East – Essex. B. Woolmer – Kent. M. Selvey – Middlesex. H. Moseley – Somerset. A. Mack – Glamorgan. R. Ratcliffe – Lancashire. G. Arnold – Sussex.

Page 56
Dennis Lillee and Jeff Thomson.

Page 57
1. Bishen Bedi 2. True 3. 1972 4. 93 mph 5. 917
6. It was a no-ball 7. His grandfather, B. Bosanquet, invented the 'googly' 8. Essex 9. Yes 10. New Zealand.

Page 53
1. Spinner 2. Iqbal 3. Madan Lal, India cricketer. The others play for Pakistan 4. They're all spin bowlers
5. Hogg 6. Western Australia 7. Wayne Daniel 8. Andy Roberts, Norbert Phillips, Mike Holding 9. Richard Collinge 10. True.

Page 59
Sarfraz Nawaz.

Wicket-keepers

Page 60
1. True. Wally Grout for Australia 2. 11 3. L. Ames of Kent, 127 dismissals 4. He didn't concede a bye
5. A. P. E. Knott 6. 23 7. No 8. Over 1000 dismissals 9. J. T. Murray in 1957 10. False.

Page 61
Knott, Evans, Marsh, Grout, Parks, Murray.

Page 62
1527.

Page 63
1. False 2. A. C. Smith, Warwickshire 3. R. W. Taylor, Derbyshire 4. No 5. Rodney Marsh, Australia
6. MBE 7. South Africa against Australia 8. 6 caught, 1 stumped 9. True. F. H. Huish of Kent, 1911
10. 1965.

The Counties

Page 64
1. 1870 2. A crown above a rose 3. Each took a wicket with first ball in first-class cricket 4. M. Hendrick, R. W. Taylor 5. D. B. Carr 6. W. H. Copson 7. 1936 8. E. J. Barlow 9. 645 10. M. Hendrick.

Page 65
Hendrick, Taylor, Miller, Tunnicliffe, Borrington.

Page 66
Lever, Denness.

Page 67
1. 1876 2. Three swords with word 'Essex' beneath 3. K. W. R. Fletcher 4. Geoff Hurst 5. 44 minutes 6. No 7. Yorkshire 8. D. J. Insole 9. True — they lost to Somerset 10. K. S. McEwan.

Page 68
1. A. R. Lewis · 2. Twice, 1948 and 1969 3. A gold daffodil 4. 1888 5. Alan Jones 6. 587–8 dec. 7. Alan Jones 8. 330, A. Jones and R. C. Fredericks 9. M. A. Nash 10. E. Davies v. Leicestershire, 1937.

Page 69
Wilfred Wooller.

Page 70
W. G. Grace.

Page 71
1. Blue, gold, brown, sky-blue, green, red 2. C. W. L. Parker 3. M. J. Procter, South Africa 4. Tony Brown 5. Champions three times, Joint-Champions once 6. Yes — 1973 7. W. R. Hammond, 1920 – 1951 8. W. H. Brain 9. M. J. Procter 10. 78.

Page 72
1. 1863 2. Twice, 1961 and 1973 3. Never 4. True 5. A Tudor rose and crown 6. 20 seasons 7. 2669 8. Kennedy, Newman 9. South Africa 10. P. J. Sainsbury.

Page 73
R. M. C. Gilliat.

Page 74
1975.

Page 75
1. 1859 2. Maroon and white 3. A white horse with 'Invicta' beneath 4. No. Six times and shared it once 5. Alan Ealham 6. Yes 7. Middlesex 8. A. P. E. Knott, T. G. Evans 9. D. L. Underwood 10. A lime tree.

Page 76
1. Red 2. 1864 3. 1928 4. Arthur Wrigley 5. H.M. The Queen 6. Frank Hayes 7. True — in 1895 8. 1816 9. Two. Nottinghamshire and Surrey 10. 371.

Page 77
Hayes, Lloyd, Scott, Croft, Engineer.

The Counties

Page 78
1. Astill 2. True 3. Grace Road 4. 1969 5. Roger Tolchard 6. Australia 7. First time 8. Worcestershire 9. No, he was born in Kent 10. William Bentley is President and Mike Turner is Secretary.

Page 79
The animal's tail.

Page 80
The centre sketch is correct.

Page 81
1. St. John's Wood 2. 331 3. Mike Gatting 4. 1964 5. John Michael 6. True 7. Gould 8. Wayne Daniel 9. 20 minutes 10. 1976.

Page 82
1. 1905 2. 300 3. All caught 4. Mushtaq Mohammad 5. Bishen Bedi 6. 10 wickets 7. Northampton 8. Sarfraz Nawaz 9. False, he played for England in 1975 and 1976 10. 8 caught and 2 stumped.

Page 83
The top badge is correct.

Page 84
Hacker, Taylor, Harris, Hassan, Johnson, Birch, Wilkinson,

Page 85

1. True. G. Gunn (father) got 183 and G. V. Gunn (son) got 100 runs, in 1931   2. West Indies, England, India, and Australia   3. 1956   4. Derek Randall   5. True   6. 17   7. Left-arm   8. Because he signed for the Kerry Packer World Series Cricket   9. Mike Smedley   10. 12.

Page 86

1. Ian Botham   2. 1938   3. 2, 356   4. Viv Richards   5. 1977   6. Two separate hundreds in a match   7. Joel Garner   8. Left-handed   9. He scored a hundred-plus on his cricket debut   10. 4th.

Page 87

The top badge is correct.

Page 88

1. The Oval   2. 1971   3. Jim Laker   4. Sir Jack Hobbs   5. 1974   6. 811   7. Seven wickets for four runs   8. True   9. Benson & Hedges Cup   10. True.

Page 89

John Edrich, Pat Pocock, Geoff Arnold, Graham Roope, Robin Jackman, Geoff Howarth.

Page 90

1. 6   2. Lancashire   3. (b)   4. Hove   5. True   6. (c)   7. Soccer   8. False. They won in 1963 and 1964.   9. William   10. For remarks he made about Geoff Boycott in a newspaper!

Page 91

Kerry Packer.

Page 92

1. Rugby union   2. 1972   3. Dennis Amiss   4. True   5. Yorkshire   6. Birmingham   7. False, Bob Willis was in the squad   8. Lance Gibbs, Rohan Kanhai, Deryck Murray, Alvin Kallicharran   9. A bear   10. 657 for, 887 against.

Page 93

No — it's a plan of Lord's cricket ground.

Page 94

1. True   2. Turnips   3. 1965   4. D'Oliveira   5. False. They won the John Player League in 1971   6. Gifford

7. New Zealand and West Indies respectively 8. 1974
9. England and India   10. A pear.

Page 95
Jim Cumbes.

Page 96
1. Herbert   2. 1962   3. True   4. False   5. 16 times
6. The White Rose   7. (a)   8. 23   9. Frederick
Sewards Trueman   10. True.

Page 97
1926.

Records

Page 98
1. 499   2. 3,816   3. 35   4. J. C. Laker for England
5. G. H. Hirst   6. True   7. 1,527   8. 1,015   9. 1,107
10. Yorkshire.

Page 99
34.

Page 100
1. Colin Cowdrey   2. 287   3. 70   4. 3 runs   5. 307
6. 8 wickets for 34 runs   7. Alan Knott   8. Rodney
Marsh   9. Colin Cowdrey   10. England.

Page 101
Colin Cowdrey.

Dates

Page 102
1. 1864   2. 1956   3. Dr William Gilbert Grace   4. 1977
5. Kent   6. 1974–75   7. 1975   8. 1960   9. 1972
10. 1977.

Page 103
Glamorgan.

Page 104
1. 1950 (Lancs and Surrey)   2. South Africa   3. 1973
4. 1975 5. 1882 6. 1973 7. 1968 8. Ray Illingworth
9. Ted Dexter 1935, C. B. Fry 1872, Jim Laker 1922,
Sir Leonard Hutton 1916   10. A mouse.

Page 105
1913, 1970.

Rules

Page 106
1. 1939 2. Yes 3. Crosses his arms back and forth at knee level 4. Umpire must revoke his call 5. (a) 6. 15 minutes 7. Yes 8. A six 9. No 10. 5 feet in width on either side of a line joining the two middle stumps.

Page 107
1. Bowled 2. Caught 3. Stumped 4. Run out 5. LBW 6. Hit ball twice 7. Hit wicket 8. Handled ball 9. Obstructing the field.

Page 108
A. Mid-Off B. Silly Mid-On C. Slip D. Square Leg.

Page 109
1. No 2. 38 inches 3. Award 6 to the batting side 4. Yes 5. (c) 6. No. He should give five runs to the batting side 7. No 8. (a) 9. Yes – in a high wind the captains may agree, with the approval of the umpires 10. Gives the batsman out.

Pages 110–111
A bail missing from wickets on left of picture. The word 'YOUR' missing from centre panel. Inverted commas missing around words TICKING OVER in right hand panel. Left foot missing from batsman on right. Lines on top of pad missing on left leg of centre batsman. Markings on back of bat missing from second picture.

Pages 112–113
Badge missing from front of sweater in second picture. Markings on back of bat missing. Laces missing on wicket keeper's foot. One wicket missing. Grass missing from beneath righthand batsman. Inverted commas missing from around word FEEL in first panel of type.

Pages 114–115
Badge missing, and pattern on front of sweater missing, in first picture. Marking on pad missing on left. The word PADS missing from centre picture. The word

EQUIPMENT missing from heading. The word BALL missing from righthand panel of type.

'My Section'

Page 116
1. 21st October 1940   2. Fitzwilliam, Yorkshire   3. Hemsworth Grammar School   4. 1962   5. It was 1963   6. 1968 v. Barbados   7. Yes – 1963   8. One hundredth century in first-class cricket   9. (b)   10. Surrey, Northamptonshire.

Page 118
1971.

Page 119
1. 1977   2. 260 not out   3. 246 v. India   4. Right-arm medium   5. 3–47 v. South Africa   6. True   7. J. H. Edrich   8. 13 – in 1971   9. 19   10. 3.

Page 120
1. 20   2. Alan Knott   3. 1964   4. No, it was also done by an Indian player in 1959   5. 1965   6. Brian Close   7. Knee   8. Broke my arm   9. Fourth   10. 4.

Page 121
2,503 runs, average 100.12.

Season 1978

Page 122
1. Kent   2. 292   3. England   4. Kent   5. New Zealand, England won both   6. Wicket-keeper Alan Knott   7. Brighton & Hove   8. Derek Underwood, Kent   9. 110   10. Andy Mack, Glamorgan.

Page 123
Burgess, Wright, Edwards, Collinge.

Page 124
Northamptonshire. Bottom of Schweppes County Championship table.

Page 125
1. Dennis Amiss   2. David Steele (Northants) and John Steele (Leicester)   3. 1,182   4. Clive Rice (Notts)   5. 213 not out   6. Sussex   7. Gordon Greenidge, Hampshire   8. One bouncer per over   9.

Hampshire   10. Phil Edmonds, Mike Brearley, Clive Radley, John Emburey.

Page 126
1. All!   2. Jeff Thomson   3. No – it was a dead ball
4. 80, Essex   5. Ray Illingworth   6. I. T. Botham
7. False. £8,000   8. Bob Simpson   9. New Zealand 1, England 1 plus 1 draw   10. Chris Tavare, Kent, 48 catches.

Page 127
Amiss, Boycott, McEwan, Randall, Procter.

True or False?

Page 128
1. True   2. False. They won it in 1975   3. False. It took place at The Oval   4. True   5. True   6. False. $4\frac{1}{4}$ inches is the maximum width   7. True   8. False   9. False. England were the winners   10. False. So long as the balls are consecutive, they don't have to be in the same over.

Page 129
True.

Page 130
1. True   2. False. He captained West Indies   3. False. Headingley is situated farthest north.   4. False. He can be stumped off a wide   5. True   6. False. He didn't captain England against New Zealand   7. True   8. True   9. True   10. True.

Page 131
False. It refers to Kent.

Page 132
1. True   2. False. Sunil Gavaskar has played for India
3. False. Frank Worrell was also knighted, in 1964   4. True   5. True   6. False. Women cricketers played at Lord's in 1976   7. False. It's a delivery by a slow left-arm bowler   8. True   9. False. The highest individual Test score is 365 by G. S. Sobers for West Indies v. Pakistan at Kingston, 1957–58   10. True.

Page 133
False. They refer to 1975.

Benson & Hedges Cup

Page 134
1. 1972   2. True   3. 20   4. A combined Oxford and Cambridge side   5. 55   6. Kent   7. Derbyshire   8. Gloucestershire   9 173   10. True.

Page 135
Leicestershire.

Page 136
1. False. They won it in 1974   2. 20   3. Lord's   4. False. It's played over 55 overs per innings   5. 3 points   6. True   7. Bedser   8. Leicestershire   9. 6 wickets   10. Alan Ealham.

Page 137
No. It's the Prudential Trophy.

Spot the Cricketer

Page 139
Jeff Thomson.

Page 140
Geoff Arnold.

Page 141
Derek Underwood.

Page 142
Barry Wood.

Page 143
Rod Marsh.

Page 144
Alan Knott.

Attention all Crossword Puzzlers!

Look out for two brand-new crossword books from Mirror Books.

Sunday People Crossword Book 2 is for all those who like to relax with relatively easy puzzles.

Womans Own Crossword Book is for people who favour something decidedly harder.

Whichever category you fall into, Mirror Books has the book for you!

Both of these titles should be available from your newsagent, price 50p. In the event of difficulty, please write direct to:

The Sales Director,
Mirror Books Ltd.,
P.O. Box 644,
Athene House,
66–73 Shoe Lane,
London EC4P 4AB.